HELLO, MOLLY!

ALSO BY MOLLY SHANNON

Tilly the Trickster (2011)

HELLO, MOLLY!

A MEMOIR

MOLLY SHANNON

WITH SEAN WILSEY

ecco

An Imprint of HarperCollinsPublishers

HarperCollins books may be purchased for educational, business, or sales promotional use. For information, please email the Special Markets Department at SPsales@harpercollins.com.

Ecco® and HarperCollins® are trademarks of HarperCollins Publishers.

FIRST EDITION

Designed by Michelle Crowe

Library of Congress Cataloging-in-Publication Data has been applied for.

ISBN 978-0-06-305623-7

22 23 24 25 26 LSC 10 9 8 7 6 5 4 3 2 1

CONTENTS

PART THREE: BABY, THIS IS IT

PART FOUR: GOOD ENDINGS

Author Note

THE EVENTS AND EXPERIENCES DETAILED HERE ARE ALL true and have been faithfully rendered as I remember them, to the best of my ability. In certain scenes the names and identifying details of the people and places involved have been changed for privacy's sake.

Though conversations come from my keen recollection of them, they are not written to represent word-for-word documentation; rather, I've retold them in a way that evokes the real feeling and meaning of what was said, in keeping with the mood and spirit of the event.

HELLO, MOLLY!

PROLOGUE: THE ACCIDENT

WHEN I WAS FOUR, I LOOKED OUT THE WINDOW OF my family's two-story house in Cleveland, Ohio, and saw a little girl on a tricycle. I was in the downstairs den, and the feeling was very peaceful. My mother was folding clothes.

I remember looking at the girl and thinking, *I really want to become friends with her.*

So I asked my mom, "How do you do that? How can I go up to her?"

She said, "All you have to do is go up, and say, 'I'm Molly,' and introduce yourself. I think you're going to have a lot of friends, because you seem like the type of person who could do that."

ON SUNDAY, JUNE 1, 1969, my mom and dad, my sisters, Mary and Katie, and I drove from our house to Mansfield, a city halfway between Cleveland and Columbus, for one of my cousins' high school graduation parties. Everyone was drinking. My dad had been working as a salesman for GM, bartering steel. He felt like he was in over his head and he was stressed-out. (My mom, who worked as a librarian at Woodland elementary school, would tell him, "Jim, you hate the job. Leave it and find something else!")

At one point during the day his sister Bernadette—Aunt Bernie—told him he'd probably had enough to drink. "Jim, that's enough," she said. "Watch it. Cut yourself off now." She tapped him on the chest with her fist for emphasis. "Be careful."

Later that afternoon, he took a nap. It was an all-day party into the evening.

It was nine at night when we finally left Mansfield, and we were two hours from our house. My mom said to Aunt Bernie, whose twenty-five-year-old daughter, Fran, was getting a ride with us, "Ugh, it's going to be a rough ride home."

Everybody came out of the party, laughing, to see us off. I fell asleep as they said their goodbyes. Years later my dad told me he'd asked my mom and Fran to drive because he was still feeling tired, and they'd said, "No, you're fine; you can drive." He asked my mom to talk to him on the ride to keep him awake.

My big sister Mary and I were in the very back of the station wagon; she was six and I was four. And our baby sister, Katie, who was only three, sat in the middle with our cousin Fran. My mom was in the front on the passenger side, and my dad was at the wheel. I remember my dad was a little bit irritated that he had to go out of his way to take Fran home. He wasn't used to going that way on the freeway. It made him nervous.

I know what happened next because as an adult my sister Mary contacted the man who'd been driving behind us. Mary was so brave to just call him on the phone one day. This man was now old and hesitant to answer her questions, but eventually he said that my dad sideswiped a car to the left, then suddenly swerved hard to the right and hit a light pole head-on. These days all light poles are breakaway poles, designed to topple on impact, but at the time they had these solid steel poles that caused terrible injuries. We smashed into a pole like that. He'd driven for ninety minutes and we were almost home.

My dad said that before he hit the pole he turned his head for just a second to ask Fran which way was the quickest, "when I felt just the slightest tap of the bumper in front of me. It was a new company car, and I remember thinking about all the paperwork I was going to have to fill out because of that one little tap. And that was it. I remember nothing after that." He blacked out.

The car was mangled badly on impact. So many people stopped to help. Firemen were called to put out the small, smoldering fire in front of the car. Another man passed the scene of the accident and stopped. By coincidence this man worked for Fran's father, my uncle John, in the car wash he owned. And he was the last person to speak with my mother.

She was lying on the ground beside our car and she asked him, "Where are my girls?" She wanted to gather her three little girls and she couldn't. I think her heart must have broken in that moment. And those were her final words. It was so strange and unlikely that someone who knew our family happened to be driving on that empty highway at the same time, enabling me to find out that my mother's last thoughts had been of Katie, Mary, and me. She died two hours later in the hospital.

My baby sister, Katie, and cousin Fran were killed instantly. Since Mary and I were in the very back, we just had a concussion and a broken arm, respectively. Katie was buried in the middle of all the wreckage. She was so small, they didn't even know that she was in the car. Officially she died of "contusions and pulpefaction of brain." I found that out as an adult when I went through my dad's filing cabinet after he died and I saw her death certificate. He'd kept this horror to himself for the rest of his life.

For so many years there was this big secret hidden in that filing cabinet.

My poor, sweet Katie, I thought. *And my dad knew this. He just buried it away.* I imagine he must have looked at it once and never wanted to look at it again.

There is no way to know exactly what happened that night, though my gut tells me he fell asleep at the wheel. But would he have fallen asleep without the drinking? It still keeps me up at night sometimes but, in the end, all that is relevant is that it changed our lives forever.

MY SISTER MARY WAS the only one who was conscious when the police arrived, so they questioned her. They asked her who'd been in the car. She had to tell them everyone's ages and where we had been. They kept saying over and over again how shocked they were at how articulate she was for a six-year-old.

When I came to, there were sirens and lots of people. I remember feeling Mary's body next to mine, our legs touching each other's, on a stretcher. And I remember being covered in a blanket that was really itchy. They took us to the hospital and they cut our clothes off. And they gave us tests.

Voices asked, "Are the lights on or are the lights off? Do you feel that? Do you feel that?" All these tests. And then they put us in a kids' ward.

I was doing really well with potty training. I had learned how not to wet myself during the night. But now I had to go to the bathroom. I shouted, "I have to go to the bathroom! I have to go to the bathroom!" I was trying so hard to hold it. I had training underpants on, and I started pleading, "I want my mommy! I want my mommy!"

Nobody came. So I just gave up and wet myself. I was despairing. I didn't know what was going on, only that everything was so dark and horrible. So even though I knew not to wet myself, I just gave up and did it anyway.

The next morning I remember waking up in the hospital, my arm in a sling. Mary was in the corner next to a large window. I was in a bed next to her, four feet away. It was a gray day. Mary remembers asking repeatedly, "Where is my mom? I want my mom!" But no one would answer her. I didn't know what to do, so I just kept my eyes on Mary, in order to follow what she was doing. She would be my guidepost. Whatever she did, I would do. But she just stared out the window and sobbed and sobbed. Then I looked around and saw all these other kids. Some were in wheelchairs. Many of them were alone, and I thought, *Oh. Wow. Well, I don't know where my parents are, but these kids have it worse than me. They don't even have anybody visiting.* I looked around. *And he doesn't have a leg, and this kid only has one arm.* I felt like Curious George when he went to the hospital.

I decided that I would take care of those kids. Since nobody would tell me what was going on, this was something I could do while I was waiting. And once I started helping them, it really cheered me up. I introduced myself and talked to them. And soon I was in a circle and getting everyone to play games.

OVER THE NEXT FEW DAYS we had a lot of visitors. People would bring us toys in the hospital, hand them to us in our beds, and try to act really cheerful. More toys and dolls than any child could ever imagine. Every day after our nap, we would wake up surrounded by even more of them. But it was not great getting all these toys.

All I could think was *Sad bed. Sad toys. Where is my mom? Where is Katie? Where is my dad?* Then I thought, *Katie must be with the other little babies in the baby section. And my mom must be with Katie and the other babies, and now I need to go see them.*

There were double doors at the top of a ramp leading out of our ward. They wouldn't let me go through those doors. But I *needed* to go out. To me it was nonnegotiable. Up the ramp, through the double doors—that's where Katie and my mom must be. So I got dressed, told the nurses, "I really need to see them," and started up the ramp.

A nurse said, "No, no, no, you can't do that," and gently brought me back to bed. My relatives didn't want to tell me what had happened. They knew they *had* to tell me but they didn't know *how.* I obviously wanted answers so they were forced into it. Finally, one of my aunts said, "I'm so sorry, Molly. Your mother and your sister Katie have gone to heaven."

I said, "Can we go visit them?"

They said, "No. No. They're in *heaven*," like it was a really good thing. *"They've gone to heaven."*

The fact that they were in heaven—this place that we couldn't even visit—was supposed to be *good* news? Heaven seemed confusing.

"Well, can we fly there? Can we hop on a plane? Can we take a hot-air balloon?" I just figured there had to be some way to *get there.*

But they repeated, "No. No."

And I remember thinking, *There's got to be a way. This is unacceptable!*

I didn't understand what was happening, so I went into a fantasy waiting for them to come back. It was impossible for me to think, *They're just dead.* It would have annihilated me. I *had* to go into a fantasy, so I just thought, *Oh, well, maybe when I get back to the house my mom is gonna be around the corner and she will pop out and surprise me or she will be over there or over there. She must be* somewhere.

I really could not accept it. I didn't know what death was. I just wondered, *Why did Mommy and Katie leave without me? I thought that my mom loved me, but now she's gone with Katie, so maybe that was all fake. Maybe she didn't really love me. Maybe I'm bad. Oh, I really wish I could see them!* That's how a kid of four's brain works. There was no way I could understand or accept they were not coming back.

My whole life changed in an instant.

BUT OUR DAD WAS ALIVE. After a bit of debate amongst the relatives—*Should we have Mary and Molly go see their dad?*—they decided to take us to see him. They thought it would be good for us. They brought us to his room with a bunch of aunts. My dad was the youngest of ten kids. A crowd of siblings stood around his bed. A mountain of cards and letters from friends was on the table beside him. He had a hole cut into his throat so he could breathe and his legs were hanging up in chains. The impact with the pole had been head-on, ramming the station wagon's engine into his lap and collapsing his chest. His legs had been pounded straight into the engine, too, so they'd had to break the whole front of the car apart to pull him out. Had he been in a smaller hospital, they would have just amputated his legs. That's how terrible it was. And his teeth were all knocked out.

He got so excited when he saw us that he tried to stick his hand into the hole in his throat so he could talk—but it got tangled in all these tubes, and then he was overwhelmed with emotion, seeing we were alive, and he started crying. It was terrifying.

My dad's best friend, Bill O'Neill, had rushed to the hospital on the night of the accident. When he saw him, he said, "That's *not* Jim Shannon!" They'd known each other since eighth grade, but my dad had such a swollen head from the impact that he was unrecognizable. The doctors didn't know if he was going to live. He'd been on the verge of being pronounced dead at the hospital. It was his orthopedic surgeon who'd had to tell my father, who was under heavy sedation, that my mom, Katie, and Fran had been killed.

And my dad shook his head and just said, "No, no, no," his body sinking into the bed.

Years later my dad told me that when he was in the hospital he dreamed he was floating up in the corner of a big room where there was a cocktail party. He was way up at the top, and his toe started dipping down. And he thought, *Oh, I can't let my toe even* touch *that cocktail party, because that's a Death Cocktail Party.* So he was trying to hold himself up but he kept slipping and thinking *DON'T let your toe even touch, because if your toe touches, it's DEATH.*

MARY REMEMBERS THAT WHEN we left the hospital a priest brought us into a little dark room, maybe the hospital chapel, and told her, "There was a terrible accident and your mom and sister died. They are in heaven." Then he told six-year-old Mary, "You have to be kind of like the mom now."

PART ONE

OHIO

CHAPTER 1

Bad Girl

I WENT TO A NUN/PSYCHIATRIST WHO ASKED ME TO DRAW A picture of my family. I drew a picture where my dad had really long arms and all of the women had chopped-off arms.

She asked, "Why don't the women have arms?"

I said, "Oh, I don't know."

I'm sure if somebody analyzed the drawing enough, everything would start to fit together.

MY SISTER AND I stayed in the hospital for a while, because nobody knew where we were going to live while our dad recuperated. Different relatives were fighting over who was going to take us.

We ended up going to my aunt Bernie's house. She was grieving because she had lost Fran, her daughter, but she took Mary and me in, and then my dad ended up getting out of the hospital a few months later and coming to live with his sister and her husband, my uncle John. My dad slept in their dining room. They put a hospital bed and bed pans in there. He had to relearn how to walk with a walker. He would practice walking slowly around their living room. It took him another year to rehabilitate. And he would always need a leg brace. When I got older I'd sometimes feel impatient at how slow he was. *Ugh*, I'd think, *I wish he could walk faster, and just normally.* I'd want to jump into his arms and sit in his lap but I had to be very careful. I could hurt him.

So we lived at my aunt's house and I went to kindergarten in their neighborhood.

One time, Aunt Bernie caught me downstairs. I had started making up little masturbation scenarios and my games were character-driven. I had tied myself to a chair with a jump rope and was acting out a fantasy about a mean, very critical, lady gym teacher who barked, "Get down on the mat! Do twenty push-ups—now!"

I then said, "Ugh!" and had to get out of the chair.

I played both roles. I stuffed my pants with clothes so I could touch myself without touching myself, using the fabric as a little layer of fat/insulation, and, pretending to be the gym teacher, yelled, "Time to get out of the chair, Fattie!"

I remember Aunt Bernie came down, saw this scene, and was so disturbed. She was obviously thinking, What the fuck is going on with this little four-and-a-half-year-old? She looked horrified. She didn't know how to handle it. She turned right around and pretended she hadn't seen anything.

THE PRIEST AT ST. Dominic School, Father Murray, was the first person who acknowledged how sad I was. He knelt down after mass one day, held my hands, looked into my eyes, and said with his thick Irish brogue, "Molly. I know you lost your mother. That's very sad. That's very hard. You lost your sister, Katie. You lost your cousin. So sad, so hard for you. God bless you."

I thought to myself, *Oh my God, I'm in love. I think I love Father Murray. He's really handsome. He has big, thick eyebrows and a kind face. Wow. This is serious. He's handsome and he understands me in a deep way.* He was my first crush.

Nobody else knew how to talk to kids. I imagined adults having conversations with each other, saying, "Just don't talk about it! Don't bring that up! It'll make her too sad." I couldn't expect them to know how deep the ache felt. Father Murray understood and I loved him for it.

WHILE LIVING AT AUNT BERNIE'S, I was walking down the street with my cousin, Jack, her teenage son. Jack was a really good artist, eccentric and daring and fun—and also grieving his sister.

A teenage girl drove up in a baby-blue convertible. She was sexy and sucking on a lollipop.

She stopped, looked at Jack, and asked him, "Want a lollipop? Want a lick? Want to come with me?"

Jack just said, *"Yeah."*

She *lured* him into the car with her lollipop. He hopped in and they drove away, really fast. It was terrifying—all mixed up in my mind with my mom and my sister being gone so suddenly. I was convinced she'd stolen him away. I just thought, *He is never, ever, ever gonna come back!*

I ran to my aunt in hysterics.

Aunt Bernie told me, "Oh, *no*, I think he'll be back."

I didn't believe her. I thought that when people went away they never came back.

KATIE HAD FOLLOWED ME around everywhere I went. She would imitate me and do whatever I told her to do. When we played house my name was always Marge. And her name was always Marge, too.

"We're going to the store. What is your name going to be, Katie?"

"Marge," she'd answer seriously, in her three-year-old voice.

"Get my purse, Marge," I'd say.

When our parents drove us to school, I would point out imaginary dragons to Katie. We pretended the Pegasus on the Mobil gas signs was one, and we would duck down in the car so that it couldn't get us. So we'd be safe.

Now I went grocery shopping with my aunt Bernie every week. She would bend down and tie my shoes and try to teach me the knots, and I'd feel this ache in my heart. I thought, *Katie should be learning how to tie her shoes, too! She should be here. She's missing all this fun stuff. She would have loved this!*

I would clench my fists and say, "That's not fair! Katie should be learning to tie her shoes!"

My aunt would make me sandwiches and I would wrinkle up my nose at her because she didn't cut the crusts off, the way my mom had done. I wanted her to do things exactly as my mom had. It upset me that she didn't. I felt that I wasn't coming home to the life that I'd left.

I would plead, "No! Mommy *always* cuts the crusts off!"

She would just patiently say, "Show me *exactly* how your mom does it."

SEPTEMBER CAME. KINDERGARTEN STARTED. I felt like I had been through a war.

On the first day of school, I was outside waiting for the bus with a few kids, and we were all getting impatient. I decided to *try something.*

"Oh, are you guys waiting for the bus?" I said. "It already came!"

They were surprised, but then they just shrugged and started walking to school. When the bus came, I had it all to myself. We drove by the kids I'd tricked and I waved to them. I couldn't believe they were that gullible. It was so fun. It gave me a feeling of deep pleasure—and distracted me from all the sadness. Being a trickster lightened the weight of all that had happened.

IN SCHOOL I MISBEHAVED around female teachers—out of fear that I'd disappoint them the way I must've disappointed my mom. And I *must have* disappointed her. I must be defective. Otherwise, why would she have left? All I could think was *I did something bad to make her leave.* So I *acted* bad around teachers to keep from getting close to them. That way I'd never get hurt again. *I'll be bad first. I'll leave you first.* I could be in control and they wouldn't surprise me by leaving. I would disappoint *them* first.

I *expected* them to leave. And that continued all through grade school. I didn't get close to female teachers. But the truth was I felt like these teachers couldn't really see how hard I was struggling. There wasn't anybody who was really thinking, *Hey, this little girl lost her mom, so she's acting out.*

Beginning in kindergarten, I sought out the worst-behaved boys and did what they were doing. Even though I knew how to draw and was a good little artist, I would just paint a whole canvas black during art class, copying what the bad boys did. But I knew in my heart that I was a good person. Even when my teacher would put me in the corner with the bad kids, the bad boys, I knew I wasn't *really* bad. *Whatever,* I thought. *She doesn't understand me. Who cares? I'll just sit here with these bad boys.*

When my sister's class was making Mother's Day cards, Mary told her teacher, "I don't have a mother. What should I do?"

The teacher said, "Oh, just go ahead and make a card anyway."

Both of us felt so let down by these teachers who were so clueless.

Later that school year I tripped and fell by the entrance to my classroom where we hung up our coats. A nail hit my knee and I wailed. As I was crying on the ground, all that I had been through suddenly hit me. I cried for a very long time, for everything that had happened to me up to that point. I really let it all out. People thought it was about the fall, but it was really about *everything.* I couldn't hold it together anymore.

I was four years old, my mother was dead, my sister Katie was dead, my father had just gotten out of the hospital, my whole world had collapsed, and there I was, trying to sing "The Wheels on the Bus."

AUNT BERNIE'S DOG, a standard poodle named Doffney, was so sweet to me after the accident. I used to lay my head on her body and take a nap. I would fall asleep on her in the kitchen after school and Doffney wouldn't move till I woke up from my nap. I would sleep on her every day and she would just stay there, so sweet.

One night Aunt Bernie washed our hair and dried it in

one of those big old-fashioned blow dryers that came down over your head. With our clean hair Mary and I watched *The Wizard of Oz*. Until the Wicked Witch of the West—played by Margaret Hamilton, who was from Cleveland—told Dorothy, "I'll get you my *pretty*—and your little dog, *too!*" And I just shouted, "*No! No!*"

She was *terrifying*.

Aunt Bernie got up and turned off the set, saying, "Molly's too upset. We have to shut this off."

It wasn't too much for Mary. She *wanted* to watch the witch. And she was so disappointed. But I just couldn't handle it.

After I turned five and Mary turned seven, Aunt Bernie threw us a joint birthday party in the park. She served pigs in a blanket and vanilla cake. Mary got sick. She was upset because Mommy would have known she liked chocolate cake.

WHEN HE WAS STILL far from recovered, my dad, who'd been practicing moving around the living room with his walker, decided to move out of Aunt Bernie's. He was fed up with Aunt Bernie's husband, John Schulte.

My dad didn't like the way Uncle John made everyone live with all these rules.

"No dogs in the living room!"

"Finish your peas!"

So when Bernie and John went to church on Sunday mornings, my dad would break the rules.

Dogs on the sofa!

Peas in the trash!

Also, Aunt Bernie had never told my uncle John what my mom had said about the rough ride home. Because if she had, he'd have asked why she'd let their daughter get in the car and ride home with my dad driving. That tension was always in the air.

SO WE HAD TO GO. My aunt Bernie told me years later that when we left her house to go home, I held on to her so tightly and screamed, crying. We moved back to our own house, on Winchell Road in Shaker Heights. And then I got held back a year in school. I repeated first grade with a mentally handicapped girl and a boy who was a future convict.

My dad didn't even tell me that they were holding me back, or *why*.

On the last day of school, standing in line at the door to leave for the summer, the teacher handed us our report cards. This boy Richie noticed me looking at mine. Everybody was shouting about how they'd passed. I was looking for my "P," but it wasn't there.

He said, "Let me see."

I handed it over and he shouted, "You flunked! You flunked, you flunked, you flunked!"

He started waving my report card around, showing it to everybody. I hadn't *flunked*. I learned later my dad had talked to the school and asked if Mary and I could repeat a year because of all we'd been through. But I didn't know that, and our dad never told us why we were being held back. Richie made it seem like I had flunked.

It was humiliating.

I felt misunderstood.

Here this kid was making it look like I was dumb, and I *knew* I wasn't dumb.

CHAPTER 2

My Sister Mary and My Best Friend (and Replacement for Katie) Ann

MARY AND I USED TO WAKE UP IN THE EARLY MORNING and watch a televised church service that counted as mass attendance. The broadcast was intended for disabled Catholics. If you were in a wheelchair and couldn't leave your house, you could get credit by watching this. It was called *Mass for Shut-Ins*. When we watched, we'd try to guess how many people would be wearing glasses when they went up to receive Holy Communion. Then we'd watch this Christian claymation show, *Davey and Goliath*, about a boy and a talking dog. It was made by the same animator who created Gumby.

I MET MY BEST FRIEND, ANN RANFT, when I was five years old. She was three and already had to wear glasses. She wore an eye patch to correct a lazy eye, too. When I first saw her, she was rocking back and forth in her crib to relax herself. I jumped in the crib next to her and started imitating her rock.

From that moment on we were inseparable. Her parents were on the road to divorce and she had three older siblings. Since I had lost my little sister, Ann was an instant replacement.

My dad always said, "Ann took over Katie's role."

ANN AND I WOULD cut out J.C. Penney models from catalogues and make paper doll families, and we'd play with Barbie dolls. We would make up elaborate Catholic scenarios for the Barbies. I would build churches and confessionals for them. And after I got a Stretch Armstrong for Christmas I made him the big, muscular, sexy priest they would have to confess their sins to: "Father, forgive me for I have *sinned.*"

"Pray for forgiveness," he'd say, protecting them.

THE TWO OF US lived in our own explosive, magical world of playing house and making up stories and doing characters and voices. We were always working on impersonations of people we knew, honing accents. We would spend the whole day talking in one character's voice. We'd be Mr. Rossi, a friend's Italian father. Or Ann's grandmother, who had this great southern Ohio accent—so country: "Now you girls go warsh yourselves up while I get the blueberry pie out of the oven." Talking in character would go on all day. Ann was so good at imitating people, not just their voices, but their mannerisms—her impressions of people were superb. It was so fun and natural. We could do it endlessly, until finally we would have to force ourselves to break character, saying, "Okay, we *gotta* stop."

As Ann remembers it, "We would play-act everything. Our houses were fifteen minutes from school, but it would take us a half hour to get home." Why? Because I was doing imitations of every single person I'd seen that day. Ann once said, "Everything was play. We'd play school, we'd play hospital, we played Barbies until we were twenty years old."

We also played this board game called Mother's Helper. My dad loved the game because it would tell us things like "Please clean the bathtub in the BATHROOM" and we'd run and go do it.

We didn't go to camp. On summer days we would just do other crazy stuff. Like wake up early, ride bikes, swim, and just excessively exercise all day long. Or take the rapid transit to the airport and watch people say hello and goodbye. We just felt life open up when we did things like that.

The best was taking the bus to the hospital to eat lunch in the cafeteria and be around the doctors. We liked to act like we were part of the hospital staff, too. I loved being in a new atmosphere, getting a tuna fish sandwich with all the doctors in scrubs and clogs, and whispering to Ann, "That doctor was just performing *surgery* on someone."

It was inspiring.

It's always good to change things up. I think that's true for anybody. And that's what hospital cafeterias were for Ann and me.

If you ever feel stuck, just go into a completely different atmosphere with different kinds of people and see how stimulating it is. There's nothing better.

ANN HAD A HARD TIME in school. Though she was so bright, she just didn't like it. But she was an unbelievable storyteller who would remember everything anyone told her.

As we got older we got into Robert Altman movies: *Nashville* and *Come Back to the 5 & Dime Jimmy Dean, Jimmy Dean*. Ann was the first person who ever said she could imagine me being in the movies.

Watching Karen Black singing "Sincerely," she said, "I could picture *you* with a Southern accent, like, doing *that*."

I said, "You really could?"

"Yeah."

She gave me so much confidence. We loved the whole Southern universe. Ann wanted to be a country singer like Emmylou Harris and live in Nashville, but she was nervous about getting up in front of people and performing.

When we were in high school, she asked me, "Can I practice my singing for you? I really do want to."

I said, "Okay."

But then she wouldn't let me look at her. She turned her back and started to sing—but she never turned around and faced me. She only wanted me to listen. And when she was finished, she wanted to know if I thought it was good. And it *was* good!

ANN, MY SISTER MARY, and I went to a Catholic school called St. Dominic's from first through eighth grade.

When anyone asked Sister Christina, my first-grade teacher, for a hall pass, she said, "Do you want to *smell* it?" It didn't make any sense but it was her way of warning us that if we misbehaved, we would get whacked.

I thought, *Sister Christina's not a happy nun. I wonder what her hair looks like underneath that veil. Is it long or short?* I was so curious. And it was strange that a beautiful young woman was dressed in drab nun garb.

But we could get extra credit at St. Dominic's if we went to the convent after school and prayed with the sisters.

So I thought, *I'll go pray with the nuns.*

Mostly I wanted to see where they lived. When I visited the convent after school, I thought, looking around, *This is so weird. The living room is so plain.* It looked like rented nun furniture.

Then Sister Christina asked me, "Do you want some pep juice?" and poured Tang into little tiny Dixie cups. I drank my pep juice as we kneeled down and prayed in her church basement. *What an interesting life for a young woman,* I thought. *Devoting her life to God. Or married to God.* She fascinated me.

Years later Sister Christina was spotted in a miniskirt with one of the boys' dads from school. He was driving a golf cart and she was riding along with him, whooping it up.

I was so happy to hear that she'd taken off her veil and left the convent. She was free!

MY INTEREST IN PERFORMING really took off in first grade when these professional choreographers, Ms. Patty and Ms. Jackie, who were also sisters (not nuns), came to St. Dominic's and taught each grade an Irish musical number with singing and dancing for the big St. Patrick's Day school show.

"Okay, five, six, seven, eight!" they said, and led us through our dance routine.

I realized these ladies were *real* professional dancers, and I'd never seen that before. St. Dominic School did not have a big budget for theater. But on St. Patrick's Day we would get costumes—prairie dresses and green vests—and put on a big show.

Ms. Patty and Ms. Jackie had jet-black hair, bright red lipstick, and wore red spandex pants. I'd wind up partially basing one of my *SNL* characters, Sally O'Malley, on them.

The head priest at St. Dominic's was Father Gallagher so for the finale all the grades sang, "G-A-double-L-A-G-H-E-R spells 'Gallagher'—proud of all the Irish that's in me!"

And I thought, *I love this. Wow.*

It was so exciting. It was always the highlight of my school year. Each grade had their own individual song-and-dance number.

On the night of the show, all the mothers showed up in the classroom to do the girls' makeup. They set up little stands. I loved the smell of the lipstick and the feeling of anticipation as I waited in line for a mother to do my makeup. I also had good instincts about show business and was very savvy at figuring out who was the best mom makeup artist.

Hmm, I thought, *her makeup is not that good. She's not gonna do a good job. Now, that mom, she's the best. Yeah, I'll go to her.* And I would tell my friends who to go to, too.

All the parents came to see us perform in the evening. It was a special night, but I couldn't fully enjoy it because St. Patrick's Day was also a big drinking day for my dad. He would go downtown to the parade and then hit the bars. That morning before he left I told him, "You're not allowed to pick me up in the classroom after the show. I'll just meet you outside on the street. Don't come to the classroom. Okay?"

I worried all day. *Oh God, I hope he's not smashed. I hope he's not drunk.* I would pray that he would come home first, take a little nap, have some coffee . . . sober up a little so he would not be too drunk for the show.

I didn't want him to come to my classroom and embarrass me.

Worry and hope.

But when I was onstage, I could tell by the way he was waving how drunk he was, slurring out to whoever was next to him, "That's my Molly."

ONE TIME, MIDWAY THROUGH the school year, our lunch cards ran out of punches. When I brought up my tray, one of the cafeteria ladies told me, "We'll let you get this *one* hot lunch for the day, but your card is out and your dad needs to pay for a new one."

I was so worried that Mary was going to have to go without food so I crumbled up a hot dog in my pocket and went out to find her on the playground.

Then I pulled the hot dog out of my pocket and held it out to her.

She said, "It's okay, Molly, someone gave me a punch on their card, so I already ate. But that's so sweet—thanks!"

We always looked out for each other.

AT ST. DOMINIC'S, I was elected president of my class two years in a row. My mother was right about my ability to make friends. I was popular.

The main reason for this was that I never wanted anyone to feel the way I did—left out, forgotten, not included—so I was good to everyone. At recess we played a game called Family. My friend Amy Wahl and I were always the moms and we drafted kids into our families. We would line up the kids on the pavement and pick families. She'd pick a kid, I'd pick a kid, she'd pick a kid—back and forth until there were no more kids. Everyone begged to be in my family because I was always the best mother. The fun mother. I made sure my family was always happy—and my kids could fly.

We played Family almost every recess near the vestibule. I would fly and my kids would follow me up into the sky and all around the parking lot.

It was a perfect fantasy.

I was the mother.

I wanted to be the *best* mother.

Then, in fifth grade, this angry boy named Billy Fox passed me a note that said, "Haha, you don't have a mother."

I had hardly ever cried before about my mom. But I broke down in front of my classmates. I just lost it. It ripped me out of my fantasy.

I remember thinking, *I do have a mother. Yes, I do! And she loves me. Okay, she's not here and she can't pick me up from school like all your mothers because she's in heaven. But I have a mom.* I wanted to get him to understand.

But really I was thinking, *Oh, no. He's probably right. She is dead.* It was a very profound and dramatic moment—the first time anybody punctured my fantasy.

The principal called my dad about the incident. That night my dad asked me if I wanted to talk about my feelings. I mumbled something like "No, that's okay." Because I was tough. When you lose a parent, you don't want anybody to treat you differently. You want to blend in. At that point I didn't want anybody to bring it up.

I was just embarrassed about the whole thing. But it made me realize how vulnerable I really was.

CHAPTER 3

My Dad: Mama Rose to My Gypsy Rose

JAMES FRANCIS SHANNON WAS THE YOUNGEST OF TEN kids and used to provoke all his sisters—Aunt Bernie and another *six*—and all their friends, too. They'd be in fancy dresses, shouting, "Jimmy Shannon, don't you *dare* spray me with that hose!" And then he would spray them.

He was *bad*. And they loved him. All women did. He was boyish and he was a troublemaker—a mischievous kid who grew up to become a dapper young man. He dressed up to go to the five-and-dime store. He would buy a movie magazine and sit at the counter with his root beer float, flipping through the pages, looking at all his favorite movie stars. He had always wanted to be an actor and perform at the Cleveland Play House but said he didn't have the confidence. And yet he was wild. Once his dog bit him and he bit his dog back. That kind of guy.

MY DAD CARED ABOUT STYLE. He wore ascots, cashmere coats, vests. I saw him as a real rebel and a radical thinker who didn't want to play by the rules. We used to go to amusement parks a lot. Once he took Ann Ranft and me, paid for himself, and made us sneak in. He didn't want to pay for us, so he said, "Just sneak around to the far side of the park where no one can see you and hop over the barbed-wire fence." It was like a test. We were little kids. And he was proud of us for making it through, though we were covered in scratches from the barbed wire. It was exhilarating.

At the mall, to make us kids laugh, my dad undressed the mannequins and threw their wigs on the floor or ripped their shirts open and pulled their pants down. He was silly and mischievous. On one occasion he adjusted one's hands so it was cupping the other's plastic boob.

Ann said, "Oh my God, your dad is so funny."

We were still little kids.

Another time, we went to see a movie at a mall after hours. He encouraged us to grab a bunch of wigs from a closed wig store. There was a big metal fence blocking the entrance and my dad said, "Stick your little hands in and see if you can steal one."

We had little wrists, so we could stick our hands through and pull out wig after wig, laughing hysterically. We wore the wigs out of the mall, cracking up.

I remember asking him, "What do you think of that girl's father?" Instead of answering, he made a "Hmm" noise and drew a big question mark in the air, like *The jury is out*. It was funny.

AND THOUGH MY DAD was super-charismatic, he could just switch if something set him off, and lose his temper. One time Ann and Mary and I were shopping with him at the Lollipop

Shoppe, where we bought our school clothes. He liked to get a deal and was picking things from the sale rack. We went up to the front to pay for our items and this young girl at the register said, "Oh, I'm so sorry, you know, this stuff is *not* on sale."

My dad said, "But I got it all from the sale rack."

The owner, an older woman, came over and said, "No, it's not on sale."

He was indignant for a moment, and then he just went into a rage. He shouted, "God damn it, then that is *false advertising*!"

Ann and Mary and I just looked at each other like *Oh, no, here he goes*. We knew we couldn't control him.

He marched back to the sales rack, looked at the sale sign, said, "*Really?*" and slid all the hangers and clothes off the rack and down onto the floor.

Then he shouted, "*This* is false advertising!"

He moved on to the next rack and did the same thing.

"And *this* is false advertising!"

He shoved both the racks over—*crash!*—and shouted, "*Come on, girls—let's go!*"

As we were leaving, without buying any clothes, he yelled at the manager, "And you're fat, you're fat, you're fat!"

We were all shocked. Ann just whispered, "Oh, *no*." Which was what we were all thinking.

As the door was shutting, my dad hissed at the clerk, "And fix your teeth!" He would always hurl one last insult, and it was always about appearance.

To say he had a temper is putting it mildly. He could be mean like Jack Nicholson's character in *Chinatown*, delivering lines that both cut down and confused people, like "You're dumber than you think I think you are."

I never knew what would set him off until it was too late.

One time Mary and I were with him, at the end of a long day at the amusement park, in a crowded tram on the way to the parking lot. He was smoking, and a woman said, "Sir, can you move away with your cigarette?"

He replied, "Can *you* move your *fat ass*? Because if you didn't take up so much space with your *fat ass*"—he waved his cigarette—"you know, maybe you wouldn't get stuck in my smoke."

SO I EITHER *ADORED* my dad or was frustrated and at the end of my rope. There was a lot of back-and-forth. I never knew which dad I would get, the one who met my needs or the one who couldn't. I'd be frustrated by him. I'd be angry with him. And then he would understand me and we would be so simpatico and so in sync and have so much fun till along came another moment of total disconnect, and I felt so alone and abandoned.

When Mary and I were little, we were completely reliant on him to be taken care of, to be *fed*. Our survival depended on him. So it was terrifying when he would fly into his rages or, even worse, descend into silence, ignoring us.

We lived in a two-family house in Shaker Heights: the top two floors and the basement were ours and the ground floor was rented out. One afternoon we heard him coming upstairs, his heels clicking one step at a time. He came through the kitchen door, looked around, and didn't say hello. He didn't say *anything*; he just gave us the silent treatment. He was mad about something. We knew the drill. So we immediately started cleaning. I don't remember what we'd overlooked that first time. Maybe Mary hadn't taken out the trash. Or I hadn't vacuumed the dining room. But it was enough to ignore us. We had to figure out what it was. This got to be a habit. He'd just come in and ignore us, sometimes for as much as a whole day. Or he'd be nice to one of us and ignore the other one, playing us against each other. We would ask him, "Daddy, are you mad?"

So from then on when we got home from school we would just start cleaning, trying to second-guess what he might look for. He would give us the silent treatment until we had fixed what we'd done wrong and he would talk to us again. That was the pattern. Whenever we heard him pull into the driveway we'd think, *Uh-oh,* and hop to it.

MY DAD WAS VERY much responsible for making me who I am. He gave me a lot of confidence. He was like the Mama Rose to my Gypsy Rose. He really believed in me, understood me, and gave me great advice, like "If you don't have a good time at a party, it's your own fault. You need to go over and introduce yourself to the person who doesn't have anyone to talk to. You need to extend yourself and go ask them questions. Take an interest. Molly, you're *naturally* good at that because you're so interested in people, and that's why you have a lot of friends." Which was the same thing my mother had noticed about me.

But then he could flip.

One time my friend Alison Earle and I were downtown at Higbee's department store, shopping, having fun. My dad loved Alison. She was easygoing, feminine, classically beautiful, with her long light brown hair—and silly. I met her in third grade and she remembers that I was the only one from the class who invited her over for a playdate, and that we put crepe paper in puddles to turn them colors. She laughed a lot with my dad. They clicked. And he was more permissive when I was with her because of how much she liked him and he liked her. Still, I needed to find a pay phone, call home, and find out if he was okay; I always had to be checking in. This time, however, I only called *once*. Alison and I did some more shopping and bought some jelly beans, and I took the rapid transit home. It was five o'clock—not too late—when I walked in. My dad was sitting in this red-and-white velvet armchair, waiting, stewing, in a rage.

He looked up at me and shouted, "You've been *downtown* not even thinking about *me*! You only think of yourself. You are *monumentally selfish*! *How dare you?*"

Even though I hadn't done anything wrong, even though I had already called him from downtown, I started to apologize—"I'm so sorry, no, no, no"—and tried to explain myself: "I didn't mean—Of course I think about you."

He repeated, "You are *monumentally selfish*!"

Then I ran up to my room and bawled my eyes out.

After a while he came upstairs and said, "Molly, I'm sorry. I worship you. I am so sorry. Don't you know I worship the ground you walk on?"

I replied, tearfully, "I love you, I love you, don't you know how much I love you? I *love* you. Of course I was thinking about you. God, I'm sorry I'm always causing you so much pain. And I'm sorry I make your life so miserable."

"No, *I'm* so sorry, I'm so sorry," he said, and he got down on his knees. "Forgive me."

Alison said I never told her about these blowouts.

I ALWAYS TOLD ANN EVERYTHING. *She* understood. But sometimes my dad could be jealous of her because she was my closest friend. He felt threatened.

If I wanted to play with Ann, there was a ritual I had to follow, even if he was in a good mood. We would sit down at the kitchen table and we would talk with him for forty-five minutes to an hour to make sure *he* was okay. Kind of telling stories, entertaining him, being silly with him. So that was the *good* scenario: him at the kitchen table, Ann there, too, all hail the king. We put in the time, laughing and having fun, and then we could go play. And all the while I'm thinking, *Can't you just enjoy that I am with my friend and you get a little break?*

But, again, that was the good scenario.

The nightmare scenario, if he was in a bad mood, was that he would just blindside me. If he knew I wanted to go play with Ann, he would pick a giant fight on some other topic before I even got out of the house to go meet her. He just became crazy with jealousy. He was afraid of abandonment, and when he was afraid he might be abandoned, he made my life hell. It almost was too much of a hassle to make plans to hang out with her.

In these moments it was just me and him. And I would experience what felt like a blackout. We'd be in the den, alone, he'd be screaming, and the whole world would contract to just us, with me crying, pleading, spinning in darkness, trying to respond to some irrational accusation, trying to get him to understand me but unable to get through.

During these fights, with my heart pounding, I could feel my brain dropping down like an elevator I was locked inside, and I couldn't get away. The arguing would pummel me into a black depression. I was in a panic, pleading for him to understand me. I was fighting for my life. And I'd be getting tunnel vision. One time, as he screamed, the whole world contracted to just the objects on his desk. I wouldn't even want to play after one of these blindsidings.

Then, when I was released to go see Ann, she would have to calm me down, because I'd be so angry and upset.

"I hate him, I hate him, I hate him," I'd cry.

And she'd listen to me. She'd comfort me as I sobbed. Even if I went on for an hour. She was like a little therapist.

One time we climbed to the top of a hill, with a beautiful view, and I cried and cried as Ann just said, "I understand. I'm sorry."

She was maternal and patient. She waited until I got it all out and then we would go play. Ann knew the drill. And it wasn't long before the cycle happened again. There was always *so much drama*. A lot of my childhood was spent listening to my dad talking about how he had lost his wife. *Not* how we had lost our mom! How he had lost his wife.

AND YET MY DAD also gave me a kind of freedom few other girls had. As a young girl there was no pressure to act ladylike: I could just be completely myself, like Pippi Longstocking. I wore whatever I wanted to wear—red and blue tights in the summertime and shorts with patent leather party shoes and bobby socks. When I had holes in my Keds, my dad said, "Good, that shows you have character. It shows that the shoes have been *worn*." My dad let me be myself. It gave me so much freedom later as a performer.

ANOTHER BENEFIT, OR CONSEQUENCE, of his anything-goes attitude was that I didn't take many baths. Because our bathroom was on the third floor of our house, it was too much for him to walk up the steps with the brace on his leg. So I also had a dirty neck. Very dirty. I remember I used to sleep over at my friend Amy Wahl's house all the time, and one of her sisters, Maureen, shouted, "Molly Shannon, your neck is filthy!" And it was *so* dirty. Black. I had a black neck because I hadn't taken a bath. *Whoa, she's right,* I thought. I hadn't even noticed.

The Wahls were a family that did normal things, like bathe. Amy's mother would make dinner every night. There were four girls in the family, and one time in front of all of them Mrs. Wahl said, "I'm going to make chicken cacciatore for dinner," and I said, "I'll have the chicken, but I don't want any of the cacciatore." The whole family really laughed. I knew before I said it that it might be funny, so I tried it out. That was the first time I made a whole group of people laugh, and I *loved* it.

Another time I went to basketball practice in a pantsuit. It was a plaid pantsuit with a matching vest, and I brought it to school in a brown grocery bag. I pulled my plaid pantsuit from my brown paper bag in the locker room, put it on, and I was Ready to Play Ball.

These other girls, whose moms had dressed them, started snickering: "I like your pantsuit."

A couple were even whispering, "Oh my God. She's the queerest."

But there I was, playing basketball, in my plaid pantsuit. And my dad didn't care. He encouraged me to be an original. So I didn't care. I always knew that I could do whatever I wanted, in certain ways, because next to me was a person who would defend me and be there for me. He even gave me insults to hurl at people.

If somebody said something mean to me in the lunch line at school, he'd ask, "What did that kid say to you?" And then he'd suggest a comeback. He was the opposite of the kind of parents you see today. One time he told me to say to an obnoxious boy, "If you had a brain in your head, you'd be *lonesome.*"

I thought, *What does that even mean? If you had a brain in your head, you'd be lonesome?* It was an old-timey insult—like something the Scarecrow in *The Wizard of Oz* would say. I liked the Scarecrow, but I never did use that one.

MY DAD ALSO TURNED to me for advice. This started around age twelve.

"Molly," he'd say, holding up some letter or contract or bill, "what should I do about this? And what about this? Read this. You're so logical, you understand." I'd look at financial documents and he'd be really, really appreciative and talk to me like an equal. I was like a little adult.

"You're so smart, Molly. Can you help me figure out these papers? You're so wise and logical." It gave me all this pride— I felt like I was a little queen. He made me feel like *Wow, I can do anything.*

"Take your time reading that," he'd say, "because I get so nervous that I'm going to make a mistake."

I thought, *I'm very capable, because he's put his trust in me to solve these adult problems.*

It was great for my self-esteem. He validated me and made me feel smart and super-competent, but then he would just turn and not take my feelings into account at all.

SINCE MY DAD HAD the role of both mother and father, he sometimes was overwhelmed. I see this even more being a parent now and wondering how he possibly did it all by himself. He was 24/7 with two little girls. There was no wife. He had no help. He had to pick us up from school, keep the house clean, take us to piano, cook us dinner, make money—he didn't have a day job but was managing rental properties and appraising houses to make ends meet—all by himself. It was a lot for a single man. So sometimes he would take a little speed.

He'd say, "I gotta catch up," pop some Dexamyl, a perfect combo of amphetamine and tranquilizer, and begin deep cleaning the whole house. My sister and I would go to school, come home, and he'd still be cleaning. He'd be cleaning, cleaning, cleaning, cleaning, cleaning—all day. Dinners with my dad were usually fun. He cooked food in plastic bags he heated in boiling water. (This was before microwaves.) It was all Stouffer's: creamed chipped beef on toast, or roast beef and potatoes. As we ate we would watch *Three's Company* and have Froot Loops for dessert. But on cleaning nights he just kept on cleaning and we had to look after ourselves. Once, after one of his all-night sprees, as the sun was rising the next morning, Mary came into my room distraught: "Daddy's still *downstairs—cleaning*!"

When we went down to the basement we found him doing laundry, sucking on a cigarette, and itching his arms—just like a speed freak. But the house was sparkling clean.

"Girls," he said, "if you want to eat, just eat on the floor. And *don't get crumbs on the ground.*"

So we all sat in a little circle and said our prayers on the floor: "Angel of God, my guardian dear, to whom God's love commits us here, ever this day be at our side, to light and guard, to rule and guide. Amen. God bless Mommy and Katie and Fran." Then we ate on the floor, and didn't get crumbs anywhere.

And when the house was finally done, he played Judy

Garland music. My dad loved Judy Garland. *Swanee, how I love ya, how I love ya!*

And . . . Everything. Was. Perfect.

From then on, "Swanee" meant the house was sparkling clean.

This was a regular occurrence. My dad would get behind, feel stressed-out, pop a Dexamyl. We called them "cleaning pills."

Hopping the Plane

ONE SUMMER MORNING, WHEN I WAS THIRTEEN AND Ann was eleven, we were sitting at the breakfast room table with my dad and talking about dares. He thought stowing away on a commercial jet—"hopping a plane"—would be the greatest possible stunt.

We said, "One day we're *gonna* hop a plane!"

We were full of bravado.

He shot back, "Well, good luck with that. I dare you."

Ann lived two blocks away, so we went and told her brother Tom, too.

He said, "You guys could never do that!"

It sounded like a challenge to us.

"Oh, yes we will!" we said.

This was when flying was really easy and you didn't need a boarding pass to get through security. We kept talking about the plan, and a few weeks later, on a summer day, we decided we were going to try it. We put on ballet outfits and put our hair in buns. We looked really innocent. Our thinking was if hopping the plane ended up not working out for some reason, we would just go take a ballet class instead. That was our backup plan. I wasn't that interested in dance, but I just loved the pulled-back hair and the pink leotards, the way the Capezio ballet shoes smelled, and pretending that I was a prim and proper little ballet dancer. For me "a ballerina" was a character I was playing.

My sister Mary was a fantastic figure skater. She really got into it, doing competitive skating in junior high and carrying on into high school. She was a beautiful skater—so athletic and graceful, meeting up with her coach and practicing all the time.

I loved inhabiting the whole world of ballet more than I loved the actual dancing.

Mr. Martin, our teacher, who was English and proper, would say humiliating stuff to me in his snotty, affected accent while explaining how to position my feet: "Molly, pretend like you are cutting a *pie* as I can see you fancy *eating*!"

WE TOOK A TRAIN from Shaker Heights all the way to Cleveland Hopkins Airport, more than twenty miles, which was already a huge thrill. All we had was a plastic bag with a change of clothes and a few dollars in it. When we got there, Ann asked me, "Where do you think we should go?"

I hadn't even thought ahead far enough to pick a destination.

"There's a flight to San Francisco," Ann said.

But there was one leaving earlier for New York, so I just took the reins and decided, "Let's go to New York!"

We walked straight to the gate and there was hardly anyone waiting to get on the flight, so I came up with a plan. I went up to a stewardess and I really innocently said, "Hi, would it be *okay* if we just go on the plane really fast so we can say goodbye to our sister?"

She said, "Sure!"

She bought it! We skipped down the jetway and took two seats near the back and ducked our heads down. We were so excited. We were savvy, tricky little operators.

I expected the stewardess to come find us. But she forgot we were on the plane. She was up at the front explaining to everyone how the seat belts worked. We started to realize that the plane was maybe going to take off. Was *actually* going to take off. With us on it. We held hands and started to pray.

"HAIL, MARY, FULL OF GRACE, the Lord is with thee. Blessed art thou amongst women and blessed is the fruit of thy womb, Jesus. Holy Mary, Mother of God, pray for us sinners, now and at the hour of our death. Amen!" Now the plane was really moving. We started to pray faster and faster . . ."Hail-MaryfullofgracetheLordiswiththeeblessedartthouamongst-womenandblessedisthefruitofthywombJesus!HailMaryfull ofgracetheLordiswiththeeblessedartthouamongstwomenan dblessedisthefruitofthywombJesus!HailMaryfullofgracethe Lordiswiththeeblessedartthouamongstwomenandblessed isthefruitofthywombJesus! Holding hands tighter, tighter, tighter, as it sped down the runway, and then we heard "*Zhzhzhzhzhzhzh!*" and the plane *took off*.

It was like *Oh my God—oh my God. Oh my God. We're in the sky. We're in the fucking air.*

WE KEPT SAYING OUR Hail Marys until the plane leveled out. Then we began to relax a bit and forgot about the steward-ess till she started going around taking drink orders. When she stopped in front of us her face turned ghost white. You could see one hundred thoughts swirling around up there. She looked like she was actually going to pass out, like her eyes were starting to roll back in her head. But she didn't say *anything*. She just collected herself, patted the front of her uniform, and said, every word super-controlled, "Can . . . I . . . Get . . . You . . . Ladies . . . Something . . . To . . . *Drink?*"

While the look on her face said, *Oh . . . mother . . . fucker. What have I done?*

"I'll have a Coke and peanuts," I answered, trying to sound really confident.

Ann asked for the same. The stewardess went and brought us our order and we just couldn't believe it.

The flight wasn't that long, but we were clenching our fists. We thought we were going to get busted when the plane landed. We walked to the front, shaking in our boots, but the same stewardess who'd let us on in the first place just smiled and said, "Bye! Ladies! Have! A! Nice! Trip!" Like a chicken with its head cut off. She looked frozen in fear. Outside of her body.

We were flabbergasted. But I guess it makes sense. I think she was afraid she would get fired—two minors, no parent, no ticket. She just let it go. She made the decision not to say a word. She looked *petrified.*

Then we were in New York City. It was a really long walk, about forty five-minutes, from the airport to the subway. We didn't know *anything*, so we just asked strangers how to get to places and they would say, "You take this train, you take that train." We picked Rockefeller Center as our first destination. I had heard about it on TV and in movies.

We snuck onto the subway, just sprinted under the turnstiles, and then we were there. I remember saying, "This is the best!" over and over. We went into a diner for grilled cheese and tomato soup, dined and dashed, saying "See you later!" as we skipped away down the street without paying. We ended up going into tourist stores and stealing "I Love NY" shirts. We just looked really sweet and innocent in our ballet outfits. We had our hair pulled back in buns. We were like two little con artists on a crime spree in New York City.

Eventually, I found a pay phone and called my dad. "We made it to New York," I said triumphantly.

"*What?* Oh my God." He couldn't believe it. But he also couldn't really be mad, because we had told him we were going to try and he had egged us on. He was definitely worried, but he was also kind of excited because he liked crazy stuff.

He said, "I don't want you wandering around the streets. Go find a hotel you can stay in and then Mary and I will drive to New York City and meet you."

Then my dad called his friend Jolene Ranft, Ann's mom, and told her that her daughter was in New York City, and she immediately broke out in multiple cold sores.

The rest of the afternoon was taken up with him calling hotels to see if they were willing to let us check into a room till he got there, or wait in the lobby—and hotels saying no and kicking us out. They didn't want to be responsible for babysitting.

None of them would let us stay. They wanted an adult with a credit card. So we got to go back out and keep walking around. We had a full day of magical New York City fun until the sun went down.

Eventually I called my dad from Forty-Second Street and he said, "All right, you've gotta come back home now. But I'm not paying for it, so try to hop on a plane back."

So we returned to LaGuardia. And when we attempted to repeat our little scam, we kept getting caught. It was easy getting onto the plane earlier, but then, on the way back, the airport was crowded. The flight we tried was packed, and as we moved from row to row people kept coming up puzzled and saying, "I'm sorry, but this is my seat."

We gave up and called my dad from the airport. He got us real tickets home. When we got back, he and Mary picked us up. He was very happy that we did it. It was like a celebration. But he was also annoyed at having to buy our tickets. He said we had to pay him back with our babysitting money. And he didn't let up on the agreement. He really did keep track of my babysitting money and took a big cut for a long time.

A FEW YEARS AGO someone asked me what lesson I learned from hopping the plane.

I said the lesson I learned is that I could get what I want with a *break-the-rules, everything-is-an-adventure, people-are-mostly-good* mentality. The world seemed open to me.

And it was the greatest day ever.

CHAPTER 5

Love and Drunks

I N A WAY MY DAD DID HAVE A PARTNER IN BILL O'NEILL, HIS best friend—and one of the kindest, gentlest, and most thoughtful adults in our lives. They met in eighth grade. Other boys were calling Mr. O'Neill a "wimp" and a "sissy" and my dad stood up and defended him. They were both smart men, with very similar senses of humor. But they were also opposites. My dad was outgoing, whereas Mr. O'Neill was reserved. My dad was slim and Mr. O'Neill was heavyset.

We went to the movies together. We took our vacations together. When we went out to fancy restaurants on vacation, places with live piano music, my dad would usually dance with me and Mr. O'Neill would dance with Mary. My sister was happy with this arrangement: she adored Mr. O'Neill. And Mr. O'Neill loved her.

Like our dad and Mr. O'Neill, my sister thought *we* were also opposites. Mary described us as "night and day, personality-wise."

But Mary was also funny—and an athlete, whip-smart, and so, so thoughtful, with a really excellent eye for interior design. People said we both spoke the same way—lots of energy and fast, really fast—and had the same mannerisms. At night we would tickle one another's backs.

But when we were kids, Mary didn't realize that the accident had bothered me, because I "seemed to go on without a care." Only as we got older did she realize that we just dealt with it differently.

Also, we both hate ticks. Do not put Mary or Molly Shannon anywhere near ticks. No.

MY DAD AND MARY and I picked up Mr. O'Neill for church every Sunday, and afterward we'd go to Sand's Delicatessen for breakfast. This tall, lanky man named John Goulet worked behind the deli counter cutting corned beef. He had the voice of a professional broadcaster and was so friendly and talkative—saying hello to everyone. We would always stop and say hi. Mr. O'Neill and my dad would split an order of eggs and hash.

Once a year Mr. O'Neill would go all-out and have us over for dinner: roast beef, mashed potatoes, and Brussels sprouts, sugar cookies from Hough Bakery—he'd do everything when he cooked for Jim and the girls. We were like family to him.

Mr. O'Neill was also an occasional blackout drunk. He was almost always sober, but once in a while he would go on benders that would last for days. He wouldn't drink for a year and then he'd slip.

On one of these benders he passed out against a store's plate glass window, shattered the whole thing, and got arrested. The shop owner was furious, and Bill had to pay to get the window replaced.

"Things like that happen to Bill," my dad said. Once he started drinking, he couldn't stop.

On vacation, Mr. O'Neill would go swimming but fail to get past the breakers and flail around in the waves. Mary and I thought it was so funny. One time in West Palm Beach, where we were staying at the Holiday Inn, he started drinking, disappeared, and then showed up at breakfast sloshed. When the waiter came over, Mr. O'Neill turned to my dad and said, "Jim. May. I. Order. A. Bourbon. Please?"—asking permission—while the waiter stood there. It was 8:00 in the morning.

My dad said, "Bill!" He was really frustrated with him. Sometimes they would get in a disagreement and wouldn't speak for months and then they'd make up. Mr. O'Neill went on benders much more often when we were on vacation.

MY DAD WAS ALWAYS taking us to school, cooking dinner, picking us up, taking us to ballet and piano. He would be completely stone sober all week—or even for weeks in a row. But then, if there was a party, he was the kind of person who would start drinking for the night and not know when to stop.

If he got stressed-out about bills—"in the red," he'd say—he might mix a vodka and tonic while he went through them. Smirnoff was the brand he liked. And when I heard a fork clicking against the sides of a glass, that stirring sound—*clink, clink, clink*—I thought, *Oh, no.* It made my heart sink.

At parties my sister and I would sneak up and sip from his glass. He'd try to hide his drinking from us. He'd pretend he was having just a plain Coke or just a plain soda. But we were suspicious he might have slipped something else in there.

We were always anxious and worried. We were always checking. We could never just relax at a party with the other kids and play.

"Go sip his drink," we'd tell each other. And if it tasted like vodka: *Ugh*.

OF COURSE, it wasn't just parties. Once a year he would go downtown and have lunch with his friend Don O'Malley. Mary and I hated those Don O'Malley lunches. Our dad usually didn't drink during the day, but when he had lunch with O'Malley, he would have a few pops.

I remember once we were watching the Little Rascals after school and he called to check in on us. I answered and he said, "Mary? Molly?" he wasn't sure who it was. "*Sweeeeeetheart . . . hewro, how you doing?*"

I covered the receiver and told my sister, "He's slurring his words on the phone."

Mary whispered, "Is he drunk?"

I whispered, "He's drunk, yeah."

We gave each other looks that said:

It's so disappointing.

It's so heartbreaking.

It was the *afternoon*.

But it was so great we had each other in these moments.

MY DAD'S INNER CIRCLE was made up of Jolene Ranft, Ann's mom, who was thoughtful but so gullible; Dick Sullivan, a very tall, very handsome guy; Francis J. Talty, sloped shoulders, tight smile, a big judge in Cleveland; and Poppy Hawley, this tiny, sexy, preppy divorcée with a beautiful daughter in high school. Poppy was literally *always* drunk. She would be in her cute tennis clothes, looking *adorable*, drunk. But she was part of the gang.

Once I blurted out to her, "Oh my God, your legs are *skinny*."

"Yes," she said, "I have very skinny legs. But they work like two thick legs."

When this gang came over, they stayed over—and drank all night. Together they would all get rip-roaring drunk.

Judge Talty was always addressed as "Judge Talty." Along with my dad, he was the ringleader in staging what they called "Catholic scenes."

"Listen, Dick," he'd say to Mr. Sullivan. "You be the bishop and I'll be the pope."

Then he said, "I absolve you, Father! In the name of the Father, the Son, and the Holy Spirit."

And then they all laughed wildly.

Poppy just shook her head and said, "You boys are *crazy*."

They *were* crazy.

Ann Ranft once caught my dad making out with her mom in their basement—and we got so excited. "Maybe they'll get married and we can be sisters!"

Sometimes my dad would wake me by calling upstairs: "Molly! Come down and play the piano!"

So I would come down in my nightgown at 4:00 in the morning.

"*Woo! Woo! Woo!*" they would all be shouting. A bunch of cheering drunks, dressed up as the pope and his bishops.

I played them T. Robin MacLachlan's "Climbing."

They applauded.

I curtsied.

I went back up to bed.

And then the sun would be rising.

But they would still be at the house. They'd order a platter from their friend John Goulet, the counter man at Sand's

Deli. He would always hook them up with a giant cold cut platter at the best price. Then they would all sit on the porch continuing their party.

Ann would call and ask, "Are the drunks at your house?"

"Yeah," I'd say. "The drunks are here." Her mom was with them, so Ann and I bonded over it. (Mrs. Ranft was not as big a drinker as the others, but she could keep up.)

"Then come over to my house. Get the cereal box and come over."

I'd grab a box of Quisp, get dressed, walk across the neighborhood, and have breakfast with Ann—to get away from those wild adults.

Another one of my best friends was my neighbor, Wendy Foy. My dad had a crush on Mrs. Foy, who was this gorgeous, really young mom who looked like Naomi Campbell. Shaker Heights was a racially mixed neighborhood—especially my street, Winchell Road, which was truly half Black and half white. There were five Foy girls, all of them natural beauties. I would sleep at their house a lot.

The Foy girls all loved my dad because he was so, so, so silly. We had a Dodge Dart Swinger and my dad would take the car out and imitate the bad driving of the woman who rented the first floor below us, one of my dad's tenants, Sally something. Stopping, starting, stalling—all over the neighborhood in our convertible. They would die laughing, the Foy girls screaming and shouting, "Mr. Shannon! Mr. Shannon! Do it again! Do it again!!" He would do full, dramatic imitations of this nervous driver. They thought my dad was the funniest. And my dad loved making them laugh and doing his impressions. I liked staying up all night with the Foy girls. We would listen to "Touch Me in the Morning" by Diana Ross, and the older sisters would smoke cigarettes and we'd all stay awake until the sun came up. At dawn Wendy and I would push our baby dolls around the block in strollers and look at maggots in the trash cans. She was a great friend.

ONCE WHEN MY SISTER and I were both at sleepovers our dad went out and drank too much at the Pewter Mug, got a DUI, and was thrown in jail for the night. He raised hell in jail. He took his cane and raked it across the bars and yelled and really created a scene.

Another time when I was in sixth grade I slept over Saturday night at my friend Amy Wahl's house and Mrs. Wahl had to break the news to me Sunday morning: "Oh . . . your dad's *not good*."

He'd been in another car accident. So Mrs. Wahl let me stay at her house all day to let him rest. I didn't get home until nine at night. When I walked in, I went up to his bed. He looked sad. I cried a little. I was worried. I had a lump in my throat. He was wearing a big bandage on his chin. Some of his teeth had been knocked out again and his chin had been cut deeply. It was really scary. And I felt bad for him. How could this happen again?

MY DAD KNEW HE had to try to get sober. He wanted to be a better person. When I was twelve he gave up drinking for the first time in a serious way. He started going to these super-Catholic Alcoholics Anonymous retreats. But then the downside was he would get all Catholic-y. We would be waiting in the car for takeout and before he would run in and get the food he would say, "While you wait, see how many Hail Marys you and Mary can say before I get back."

Usually we would both laugh and think, *Oh God, it's just too religious. We're not going to say Hail Marys while we wait for our hamburgers at Manor's.*

But sometimes we would have to say the Hail Marys. Then at night he would kneel down on the floor by the side of his bed and say his prayers. There was this big beautiful framed photo of my mom in her wedding dress on his nightstand with a rosary draped across it and the mass card from her funeral.

He was always "working his AA recovery program," trying not to drink. Avoiding selfishness, seeing the best in people. He would write notes in the back of his small black Alcoholics Anonymous prayer books to encourage himself. He filled them with little motivational aphorisms:

One day at a time

Make the most of this day

No name dropping

No gossip

Listen to others with interest—concentrate on what they are saying

Don't try to impress people—keep mouth shut

Do *not criticize* others

Respect all as they are

Be humble

Think of all favors others have done for you

Listen—Pay attention *to others*—*LISTEN*

He would meditate on that stuff daily.

But when he got asked to lead AA meetings, he would be nervous. So I would coach him.

"Just tell the truth. Tell your story. It will be good."

"Oh, Molly, thank you!"

WE WENT TO MASS every Sunday at St. Dominic's. Mary and I would sit in our pew behind the perfect little Catholic families with a mommy and a daddy and all their kids dressed in their Sunday best. I would study the way the moms would act with their daughters. One time during mass, to make Mary laugh, I imitated one of those perfect moms and pretended Mary was my little daughter. I lovingly stroked Mary's shoulder length brown hair. Then I put her hair behind her ear and said, "Oh, darling! You look so pretty! You should wear your hair like that all the time—behind your ears," pretending to be her doting mother. Mary was cracking up! She thought it was so funny. Then, playing along, she started doing it to me: "Oh, honeybun, *your* hair looks so nice. Pull your hair back like that." She would do it to me and I would do it to her and we would pretend to be each other's mother. It was so relaxing and silly and it felt *so* good. Church games!

When my dad met a stranger he liked, he took an interest in who they were. He used to pick up hitchhikers. There were a lot of drifters in '70s Ohio, and we got to know as many of them as we could. He didn't judge them. He would always give it up for anyone who had skills or experiences that he didn't have. And people would really open up. Adults at cocktail parties. My friends. He was genuinely interested in everyone, and remembered names and asked questions and *took notes*. He was adorable. So cute and funny. He really liked people. Especially intelligent people. He was moved by intellect, always wanting to learn something he didn't know. And he was also very emotional. When I would say, "Daddy, I love you," he would mouth back: "No. I"—pointing to himself— "love you"—pointing to me, and then he would get all choked up. And if something was really touching to him, he would always be fighting back tears. He had a very big heart. And when he would lose his temper, he would feel remorse.

My friends never felt judged by him. They would open up to him in a way that they didn't with their own parents because he was so easygoing and open-minded and he had an alternative view of things. You could tell him anything without feeling judged. He was genuinely interested in what you had to say. He would always ask them questions about themselves.

CHAPTER 6

Swimming to Juvie

MY DAD ENCOURAGED MISCHIEF.

He'd make Mary and me *pretend* to answer fake phone calls. He wanted us to be utterly convincing. We called it the Telephone Game. He showed us how to do it first. How to make it real. Then it was our turn. I'd answer, "Shannon residence. This is Molly. Uh-huh. Yeah. He's right here. Oh, no, no, you're not both—"

"Freeze. Stop," he'd say. "Start over. That seemed fake."

So I'd try again. "Hello! Yeah? Yeah, I'm here with my dad, uh-huh. It's no bother. Okay. Okay. I'll put him on."

"Better."

I got so good I could really trick friends when they came over, even though they never heard the phone ringing.

"Hello? Hello. *Yeah.* Alison? Alison *Earle*? She's here. You want to talk to her? Sure. Okay, I won't say anything." I'd give Alison a *This is weird. What is this person talking about?* look to draw her in. To make it mysterious. *Who is that calling for Alison?*

It had to be 100 percent real. No acting. It was the best exercise, and how I first developed my skills. It was the Jim Shannon school of *real* acting.

ON CHRISTMAS AND HIS BIRTHDAY, our dad didn't want gifts. He wanted cash. Mary and I would compete to see how much we could hand over.

I'd ask Mary, "How much are *you* giving him?"

"Two hundred."

"Shit. I'm only giving him one-fifty."

And when we gave him our money he'd say, "*Thank. You.*" Like that was his due.

When he was supposed to treat our friends to a meal, he'd tell us, "I don't want to have to pay for your friends."

We would beg him, "Don't take money from our friends, please. Just *treat* them, because *their* parents treat *us* when they take us to restaurants."

But if a kid ever held up some money to pay, saying, "Oh, here, Mr. Shannon, take this," he would snatch it—*snap!*— really quickly. And that was it. The money was *his*. And we were so embarrassed. To prevent that from happening, we started to give him our babysitting money ahead of time so we could make it *look* like he was paying for our friends.

AS I GOT OLDER scams began to interest me on my own. I saw that they had potential. I started trying to think of fast ways to make money. One Christmas I realized, *Caroling for charity! Oh, singing with a cup!*

I told Alison my idea and together one snowy night we knocked on doors, sang "Silent Night," told people we were donating to some made-up charity, and just took their money. And we made a wad of cash. We went house to house and ended up making about $200. And then we went and sat at the bar of this hotel restaurant on Chagrin Boulevard and ordered Coca-Colas to celebrate.

I thought, *Going into people's living rooms at Christmastime and putting on a little holiday show is the easiest way to make some fast cash.*

ONE DAY WHEN ANN and I were babysitting, we decided, "Hey, let's get this cute little three-year-old boy a new outfit!"

So we took him downtown, changed him right in the aisle at Higbee's, and walked out with free clothing. It was so easy.

Then I decided to shoplift my own bra. I was too embarrassed to ask my dad to take me to get one, so Ann and I went and stole bras downtown at the May Company. And then my dad saw me with a bra and gave me this questioning look.

I said, "Oh, our gymnastics teacher said it was a requirement and gave us these."

He just said, "Oh, okay."

I felt embarrassed, because it was so girly and I just knew it was something a mom should do for a daughter.

To be a successful shoplifter, you just had to act like you weren't doing anything wrong. It was acting. We would take a huge bag and shoplift our way through a store, taking what we wanted, even asking salespeople for help finding things. We used to call it "swimming."

ONE SUMMER AFTERNOON, sitting on our porch, I asked Ann, "Want to go swimming?" My dad had given us the aqua Chevy Malibu convertible.

Ann replied, "Yeah, let's go swimming."

We both said, "Back-to-school shopping!"

So we drove to Value City and just loaded up on stuff.

We brought big purses in. After stealing as much as we could carry, we went through the checkout line to each buy something cheap.

It was a big haul: we had really stolen *a lot*. Ann went through the line first and was exiting the store as I paid for the little token thing I had brought up to the register.

And just as I was thinking, *Oh, good, I'm gonna make it,* a huge security guy clapped his hand on my shoulder and said, "Come with me." He had leaned across all these shoppers in the checkout line to grab me.

I thought, *Fuck.*

As I watched Ann make it to the car, I kept thinking, *She'd better be caught with me.* I just didn't want to be by myself.

The security guy took me in the back and began interrogating me.

He said, "We know what you did."

I was a punky, tough kid, into the whole idea of bad girls and juvenile detention. To me it seemed like fun being in that sort of trouble.

I looked at this security guy and thought, *Fuck you, you don't fucking scare me.* I wasn't afraid. I thought he was a real asshole.

I said, "Arrest me."

So he called the cops.

Then I said, "Okay. So we stole. We're bad kids. Go ahead, handcuff me!"

Meanwhile, out in the parking lot, it was dawning on Ann that maybe I'd been caught and she was saying to herself, *Oh, shit, shit, where's Molly?* Where's Molly? *Oh my God! Oh my God!* and in heart-pounding terror got in the car and started quickly hiding what she'd stolen under the seats. Then—

boom—two police cruisers surrounded her, and the cops started pulling stuff out of the Malibu and asking, "Do you have receipts for this?"

She said, "Uh, I was jus—"

And she got pulled out of the car and brought back to where I was.

Yay!

THE THOUGHT OF JUVENILE detention truly excited me. I thought, *Yeah, I want to be with the bad girls. This is so fun! Me and Ann are bad together.* The whole thing was exciting. *Maybe we'll go to jail or to juvie!* I *wanted* to go. I felt excited and curious about it.

We went to the police station and got fingerprinted.

They put us in different rooms. Ann called her mom.

Through the walls I heard her say, "Hi, Mom, it's Ann. . . ." Then answering her mom's question she wailed, "*Police station! Shoplifting!*" Her cry reverberated through the place.

Then my dad arrived to get us and the sound of him walking with his leg brace echoed through the halls. *He'd* taught me to be wild, but now he was pissed that we had taken it that far. After that, Ann and I were banned from going to stores together. And they made us go to Shoplifters Anonymous meetings, which we just thought was hysterical. We loved it! As long as we could be together it was all great. Shoplifters Anonymous was even funner than shoplifting. I remember thinking it was so funny going to meetings and sharing with other bad girls.

But it wasn't funny.

Mr. O'Neill happened to be in the hospital at the time,

recovering from some routine surgery, and we went to visit him. My dad had already told him what had happened. When I walked into Mr. O'Neill's hospital room, he looked at me, disappointed, and just said, "Oh, Molly."

And I felt so ashamed. I never did steal again after that.

CHAPTER 7

The Lullaby of Broadway

FOR A LONG TIME I USED TO HAVE FANTASIES ABOUT BEING signed by a big New York City talent manager. I thought that from the moment a manager signed me I would of course only eat salads, because I would—as a professional actress—have to be very concerned with keeping myself fit. My fantasy was that I would be signed by a manager, eat lots of healthy green salads, and become a professional actress.

When the All New Mickey Mouse Club came to Ohio, my dad said, "*You* should audition."

He drove Mary, Ann, and me way across town. But we missed the Mickey Mouse Club audition and somehow I wound up auditioning for something completely different that I *thought* was the All New Mickey Mouse Club. It *was* an audition. I *did* have to sing a song. There was a piano and I went right into "Tea for Two."

When I was done they said, "We want you!"

I still thought it was the All New Mickey Mouse Club.

But it was something called the Little Rascals, or the New Little Rascals—this terrible show that went around to carnivals and Greek restaurants. It was that low-budget. And the woman who was in charge of my group was another hard drinker.

Being in the New Little Rascals was still *kind of* good, because I got up in front of an audience, and I would sing and people would stay and listen. It was good practice performing live. But it was a crappy show. I really thought that I'd gotten into the All New Mickey Mouse Club instead of some local, dumpy, carnival-and-restaurant Little Rascals thing. My dad drove me all across town to perform in these shows.

One time we were in a backyard, getting ready for a performance, and the woman who ran it was wobbly drunk at ten o'clock in the morning. I was riveted. I was so much more interested in studying her as a character and thinking about her and getting an opportunity to follow her and watch her than I was in singing "Tea for Two."

I could not take my eyes off of her. She fascinated me. I thought, *This lady is calling the shots? This is not good. This is worth everything.*

There were only six or seven of us in the group. One of the girls was named Connie, and her mother would help me get ready, because she knew I didn't have a mother. Connie's mom sewed red sparkles on the white polyester one-piece jumpsuit/short sets we had to wear so we all looked the same. We also had to wash our hair before the shows. I distinctly remember Connie's mom washing my hair backstage, and when she touched my head I thought, *Oh my God, I love this. These are things I like about showbiz.*

It had been so many years since a lady—or anyone—had washed my hair. The braces on my dad's legs kept him from walking upstairs to give us baths. This was why I had the dirty neck, though he loved taking us to Dominic's, the hip new Beachwood hair salon, to get us pixies or Dorothy Hamills.

AFTER THE NEW LITTLE RASCALS, I auditioned for Heights Youth Theatre, a fantastic group that did big musicals like *Alice in Wonderland* and *Oliver!* for giant local audiences filled with families and kids. It was a very professional, almost pre-Broadway theater group.

Originally the shows were in a theater at Wiley School in University Heights. Then they moved to the Front Row, a 3,200-seat theater-in-the-round where comedians and musical acts like Joan Rivers, Richard Pryor, Bob Marley, and the Jackson Five performed.

When I auditioned and got the lead part of Dorothy in *The Wizard of Oz,* it was significant, not just because these were giant productions with sold-out audiences, but because almost everyone else was older, seventeen, almost adults, while I was eleven. Many of us went on to professional careers. Our piano player for *The Wizard of Oz* was Jim Brickman—Jimmy, who'd later record five gold records. Heights Youth Theatre was this big arts organization with the best kids in Cleveland auditioning and I started getting recognized around town. I would go to the shoe store and little kids would say, "That's the girl who plays Dorothy."

I had a big, *thick* script to memorize. I loved the smell of the mimeographed pages that they gave us on the first day of rehearsal. And there was this professional costume fitting. The girl who'd played Dorothy before was eighteen, and since I was so much younger and littler, they had to take in the dress a lot. Especially in the boobs: the prior Dorothy was basically a woman.

But what I liked best about acting was that the theater kids were really affectionate. I was in fifth grade and had been in Catholic school till then. I was meeting these other kids at Heights Youth Theatre from predominantly Jewish backgrounds. *Oh,* I thought, *there's a really big difference between Jewish kids and Catholic kids*—though I wasn't sure if it was because they were theater kids or because they were Jewish. But these were *my* people.

All the kids were just so warm. We would all braid each other's hair. We would have massage chains. There was all this touching. That's really what drew me into showbiz: everyone sitting on the floor in a group, giving massages as the girls brushed and braided and played with each other's hair. I just loved the way everyone was so affectionate. The warmth that I was missing from a mother I got from these theater kids, and their affection.

I thought, *This is pure heaven.* And then I met the boy who played the Scarecrow, the only other cast member my age, and fell madly in love. His name was George Cheeks, and I'm still so close to him.

George was half African American and half Greek. His mom's side is related to George Stephanopoulos. His parents divorced when he was little, and his mom, Jennie Cheeks, was a famous DJ for WMMS, Cleveland's big rock station. George had that same charisma, and he wanted to kiss me. I had such a crush on him. One time my dad and sister and I bumped into him behind the Dairy Queen, where they had this giant slide, and he asked me if I wanted to go down in a potato sack with him. I was nervous about doing it but my dad said, "Go!"

In the summertime George and I went swimming in Lake Erie and he said, "Let's take our clothes off together."

I thought, *Oh my God. Take off my clothes! Oh, my beating heart!*

We kissed underwater. I really to this day believe that kids can fall in love, because I felt such deep love for George.

I had never felt anything like that before. Mary and I had gone to a formal ballroom class at a place called Mrs. Batzer's Dancing School. It was a pre-cotillion thing for the rich kids, but our dad got us in. The boys would wear jackets and ties and sit on one side of the room and the girls wore white gloves and pretty dresses and sat on the other side. The boys would always cross the room and ask the girls to dance. A piano player named Bubbles played while we danced the foxtrot. And then we would have fancy parties at country clubs with boy-girl dances. There was this one chubby boy called Mickey Covington who would make a beeline to me and say, "May I have this dance?"

And I thought, *Mickey Covington again.* Because he would *always* pick me. Always, consistently, for the three years of dancing school, he asked me to dance.

And I would think, *All right. Fine,* while looking over his head at some other boy across the dance floor and thinking, *I wish that boy would ask me to dance.*

But then, finally, during a Batzer's party at a country club, after dancing with Mickey, we went and sat with my friends and had some Cokes. I was really comfortable and we were laughing and talking and I realized, *I think I really like this Mickey Covington. He is so sweet and thoughtful. Good manners. Good conversationalist. He asks me questions about myself. I ask him questions. I feel so comfortable. And if I didn't give a shit what anybody thought, I would just enjoy having a Coke with Mickey Covington. He likes me. I like him. There is nowhere else I want to be right now but right here with Mickey. Just embrace the guy who likes you, who adores you, who consistently comes after you. Don't go look for the guy over there who's not paying any attention to you or the guy you have to chase after.*

And I brought some of that same feeling to my relationship

with George—that comfort—which is why, when the romance was over, we stayed close.

GEORGE HAD INTRODUCED ME to one of his best friends, Debbie Palermo. The three of us became a trio. Debbie went to public school in Cleveland Heights with George, but then George transferred in tenth grade to the private school where I went after St. Dominic's, Hawken School, where the ratio of boys to girls was something like 70–30—so it was a big deal to get in if you were a girl. They offered me a great financial aid package. The whole atmosphere was really preppie, and there was a lot of homework.

Hawken also had a foreign exchange program and I stayed in Paris in the spring of my sophomore year. Then two French exchange students, Amelie and Beatrice, lived with us the following summer. Amelie was cool and Beatrice was nerdy. But they were both very French and came from these upper class families. Amelie lived in a mansion on one of the fanciest boulevards in Paris. In Paris I was supposed to stay with Beatrice and live on her family's houseboat in Neuilly on the Seine, but she had cats, and I was allergic, so I stayed with the woman who ran the exchange program. I learned how to speak French by practicing with her little three-year-old daughter. She spoke simply and I could practice while playing with her.

But my dad was miserable the summer we hosted those French girls. He couldn't stand that they were so much more sophisticated than Mary and me. They were just very confident, wearing scarves, turning up their noses at his plastic bags of Stouffer's, and getting out all the pots and pans to cook. It drove him crazy how they dressed so well and talked with such confidence and took over our house. He had to host them because that was part of the deal with the exchange program. But he was competitive.

My sister and I would crack up because he was in such a bad mood the whole summer. Just *cranky*.

They would make all this French food and then Amelie would throw it back up.

She was so *casual* about it, even showing me how. Finger down her throat—"Bleeeeeh!" into the toilet—and then, "*Voilà! Comme ça! Vomissez! Là-là!*" in her cute French accent, whistling while she mimed fingers down the throat.

And Amelie would kind of boss our dad around with all her ideas.

"Meester Shannon, today we leave Clevelahnd. We hire a car and drive to Cheecahgo for the day."

We got stopped by the police once for speeding and Amelie said to us, "*Ahhh, parlez français, parlez français!* Speak French, speak French!"

So when the cop came to the window and said, "D-R-I-V-E-R-S L-I-C-E-N-S-E," I told him, "*Je ne parle pas anglais.*"

Then we all spoke French till he let us go.

We did stuff like that for the whole summer.

And my dad was just consumed with jealousy. But for Mary and me it was a fun summer. We loved that we got to go around in the Chevy Malibu convertible with these wild and sophisticated French girls. They dominated town. Amelie was a natural beauty, in an effortless way. Beatrice was more of a tomboy. Amelie couldn't care less about boys, but the boys fell at her feet. Beatrice was almost like her girlfriend. They were thick as thieves.

GEORGE AND DEBBIE WERE obsessed with Bette Midler, and particularly her film *The Rose* and its soundtrack. They were also dying to see *Making Love,* a scandalous movie at the time with a gay subplot, so I joined them. We all adored drama, and Deb and George were both in the closet back then, which made it extra fascinating. Deb told me later that she knew she was gay at this time and that she was in love with Bette. Then she dated George briefly and imagined he was Bette. She and George had so many loves in common that she fell in love with him. They'd met in class at their public school when someone shouted "Janis Joplin" and George shouted back, "The Rose!" Their adoration of Bette Midler brought them together.

But in high school George wasn't out of the closet yet. "I couldn't admit it to myself," he told me. And though our feelings were romantic when we were little, we went to different schools for junior high and the first two years of high school. Then when he came to Hawken as a junior he wanted to date me. I remember we went out one night downtown for dinner. "Every Little Thing She Does Is Magic" by the Police was playing, it was snowing, and we kissed a little when he dropped me off. But the next week at school I wrote him a sweet little note saying that in my gut he felt more like a brother or a friend and that it wasn't right. He wrote me back saying he was disappointed but he understood.

Debbie was from a big Italian family. I would go to the Palermo house all the time for big dinners: rigatoni with sausage, spaghetti and meatballs. I loved that house because everybody was so warm and affectionate and their grandma lived with them, too, all these generations together. There was all this cooking and love and laughter. Deb's family was very supportive of me. I also became very close to her little brother Mike and started to think of him as my adopted little brother.

Mike told me I was "the only friend of Debbie's that genuinely asked me questions about my life and truly seemed to care about my answers. I remember crying when you left because I couldn't stop thinking about you and how all I wanted to do was keep talking."

DEB, GEORGE, AND I took a trip to New York when we were just old enough to be traveling on our own. We got a bus from Cleveland and stayed at the Milford Plaza, right in Times Square, where you could get a room, dinner, cocktails, and breakfast, all for $43. They had an ad that was always on TV, showing bellhops, chambermaids, waiters, concierges, all carrying bags, making beds, lighting desserts on fire, and answering phones to "Lullaby of Broadway."

EVERYBODY AT HAWKEN HAD money and flew down to Florida for vacation. My dad didn't want Mary and me to feel left out, so, even though he was deep in the red and struggling, he sent us to Palm Beach by ourselves. We stayed at this motel for elderly people called Testa's. I think it's been torn down, but in the '80s it was *the* cheap place where lots of older women did long-term living. The rooms didn't have TVs, so Mary and I watched *General Hospital* every day on a communal TV down in the lobby with all the old people.

Those were *sweet* memories with my sister. We both liked Testa's because it was like a step back in time. But we really bonded over the fact that we wanted to get *tan*. We knew that if we went back to school tan, people would think we were rich kids who could afford to go to Palm Beach or Boca for vacation.

We also used to walk over to the snazzy hotel, the Breakers, swim in their pool, and look at all the actual rich kids. They were just swimming in this giant pool beside the ocean, eating cheeseburgers, and charging them to their rooms.

God, I thought. *They're lucky to be rich. They can eat burgers by this big, fancy pool and take it for granted.*

My dad did come with us on other trips to Palm Beach and took us to this fancy restaurant, with live piano music, Doherty's. We got baked potatoes and the best roasted chicken.

We also had lunch with a woman my dad knew from Ohio. I told her I was planning to move to LA to become an actress and she said, "Oh, honey. You *can't* go to Los Angeles. Not without your SAG card."

As if it just wasn't possible.

At first I thought, *Really? Oh God.* But then it just made me mad. My reaction was: *I'm not listening to* that.

I always dismissed that kind of advice.

I was tough.

MY DAD WOULD OFTEN take trips to Palm Beach by himself and stay at Testa's. Usually he wouldn't drink during these trips. He would have years and years of sobriety. But when my dad *was* drinking, he loved piano bars. One time he met a lady who was traveling around in her station wagon, looking for work, with a handwritten sign that said, "Have Piano— Will Travel!"

She was the kind of character that I eventually did on *SNL.* A woman in her sixties performing with her piano at resort town restaurants. An old showbiz gal looking for *work.*

"Have Piano—Will Travel!"

Those kinds of ladies.

He took her out once and after that she would bang on his door: "Jim, want to go get dinner tonight?"

He called home to tell us about her.

"Oh my God, she's driving me crazy," he said. "She keeps knocking on my door to see if I'm free. I just want to tell her, 'Give me some *space!*'"

Another time he met Elizabeth Taylor. She was doing *The Little Foxes* at the Parker Playhouse in Fort Lauderdale. Before big shows would go to Broadway or London, they'd try them out in small towns to iron out the wrinkles.

He *was* drinking that time and managed to get invited into her dressing room after the show, saying, "I *know* Ms. Taylor."

She let him in, saying, "Have a drink and get out."

On another of these trips, just me and him, my dad drank too much. He dropped me off after dinner and then he went back out to the clubs in West Palm by himself. After he returned *late* late, I woke up and saw him sitting up on his bed with a cigarette dangling from his lips, a big ash hanging off the end of it. He hadn't noticed the ash and was just dozing off. I took the cigarette, put it out, snapped him out of it: "You could've set this place on fire. Go to bed!"

It was dawn. I felt so mad I ran, ran, ran, ran, ran, ran as fast as I could down the beach, crying to get my anger out. It was a release. I didn't know what to do and it felt good to just run and run and run and run and run and run as fast as I could. Hours later, after he woke up, we sat down and had a serious conversation.

I said, "It's so upsetting to see you so drunk like that. It's scary. Please, I beg of you, go back and talk to those people at AA."

My dad was not defensive. He felt terrible. "You are right, Molly," he said.

I got through to him and he listened to me. But it also felt so unfair that I even had to say it—that it had to come to this.

IN HIGH SCHOOL I always had to babysit to make money. And I missed a lot of parties. My dad would tell me, "Oh, it's just a party. Don't worry. There will always be more parties."

But I had this anxious feeling about missing parties. On the occasions when I did go, I couldn't get there fast enough.

I would longingly think, *The love of my life might be at that party and I need to get there* now.

And what my dad said about parties *wasn't* true. High school ended and there were no more of those parties.

I LEARNED HOW TO be comfortable with Mickey Covington, though George Cheeks was my first true love. But before Mickey and George, I loved bad boys—like, literally, convicts.

I started liking bad boys when I was little.

When Mary and I were kids, our dad would take us to juvenile jail and visit the boys who were locked up there.

My dad told us, "We're going because they don't have any family, and they need a big-brother type. They need somebody to listen to them and talk to them."

The jail was fenced in with barbed wire, and it had a big smokestack. I remember there was smoke coming out of it as we walked up, and I wondered, *Do they send the really bad boys up in smoke?*

I even asked my dad, "Do they burn them and then smoke them out?"

We brought the bad boys brown bags of cigarettes, Lay's potato chips, and Doritos. We would sit with them and talk, and they'd smoke, and my dad would listen. It was one of his ways of being a good Catholic. The prisoners were young, no more than seventeen years old. They wore T-shirts, and I liked their cigarettes.

My sister and I said to each other, "This is fascinating."

And I thought, *Wow, these boys are bad!*

Like a boy who'd been held back in first grade with me, Patrick Byrne. He was friends with Ann's brother and one time when we all went to Mrs. Ranft's cabin, Patrick just sneaked into bed with Ann and me. She felt his hairy legs and shouted, "Patrick!" He was very developed to have such hairy legs. We hadn't gone through puberty.

For some reason my dad called him Marty, and my dad thought he was *amazing.*

"Oh, that Marty Byrne—he is just so charming."

I just thought, *Patrick Byrne is bad.*

He *was* very charming to adults but would then turn around and do these deviant things, like Eddie Haskell from *Leave It to Beaver.*

Patrick also had redeeming qualities, even when he was technically bullying people. When he saw the mean note about my mom being dead that Billy Fox passed me, he organized a bunch of kids from our class to kick Billy's ass. They cornered Billy, who was weeping, cowering, and Patrick said, "How could you do that to Molly? That is *terrible.* If you *ever* hurt Molly again in any way I swear to God, I will fucking kill you."

He has my back, I thought. *He's got balls.*

I felt protected. Alison and all the kids hugged me and said, "It's okay, Molly."

Billy was scared to death.

Once Patrick used a tree in my backyard to scale three floors and break into my bedroom window. I loved it. He came crashing in, pulled down his pants—penis totally erect—and said, "You know, hold it!"

I wrote in my diary, "Oh yeah diary here's some juicy info I have a mad crush on Patrick. But I don't think he really likes me (especially my chest) but he does call on me once in a while. My best friend is Alison. I love my daddy and my sis. Ann Ranft is my other best friend. My dream for today is to be a fantastic gymnast. Well that's all bye."

I just really wanted Patrick to kiss me. I had a fantasy that we could be like Bonnie and Clyde. But at the same time he wanted to do all this dirty stuff, like pull down his pants and attack girls.

I would have loved to have gone on dates with him but he was too busy attacking other young women. He really enjoyed breaking into my babysitting jobs.

He was *really* bad. His dad was a cop who used to beat him with chains. And his mother was completely passive because she was so scared of her husband. He later accumulated quite an aggravated robbery record and went to prison for trying to kill his girlfriend's father for money. He would write me letters from prison about his tattoos. When he was in prison he changed. Hardened. It was a scary change. He went from a funny, handsome, charismatic kid to a convict. It was scary how fast he turned bad. He got chain link inked around his neck. At one point he broke out and was found with an arsenal of weapons in his house, went back to jail, escaped again, and was caught with more weapons in his car.

In one of the letters he sent me from prison Patrick described his life:

I must explain I can't tell you my crime in detail because my case is still being pursued by detectives in Shaker. No person knows what really happened. I'm still being questioned and writing statements. I can tell you my charges though

1. *2 counts of attempted murder*

2. *aggravated burglary*

3. *grand theft*

So you see I'm not the angel I was thought to be Molly. Your partially right about my innocence.

Things will work out for you. I hope. Life in here has given me a different aspect of life out there in general. You'll see the different person I am. People will be on guard of me, but I still have a good personality.

This was the type of person I was attracted to when I was little. He made my heart pound. He was dangerous, a *real* bad boy. Though later I wrote in my diary, "I've decided I don't like Patrick anymore because he has no patience or courtesy."

I HEARD HE WAS eventually killed in a high-speed car chase on his way to murder a girl. This was a real person!

CHAPTER 8

Leaving

I N HIGH SCHOOL THERE WERE ACHIEVEMENT TESTS FOR admission to special classes, which were helpful for college. And I was interested—but to take the tests I needed to bring a check into school. I couldn't pay in cash. My babysitting money was no good.

I didn't bother asking my dad, "Oh, could you write a check for me to take this test?" because I knew it would just stress him out. By then I had learned to not ask for too much: if he did give me something, he would hold it over me. There would be all these strings attached. It made me very independent. I just wanted to make my own money.

My dad didn't give a *shit* about school. He was the total opposite of any parent you would ever meet. His opinion about cheating on tests was: Try to cheat, if there is any way. He always told me, "If you can cheat or find the answers or give yourself an extra day, do that."

In tenth grade I was stressed-out studying for a test and he asked, "Can't you find a copy of the test so you can cheat? Or stay home from school and study more?" He did not care about grades. He felt that a combination of social ability, street smarts, understanding how to make a buck, asking people questions, being charming, and showing an interest in others would get you a lot further in life than academic achievement. That's what he encouraged in me—what I guess my mother saw in me from the beginning.

Sometimes I would be up till 3:00 in the morning studying down in my basement, drinking Taster's Choice instant coffee to stay awake, and he'd say, "Molly, *please*, go to bed, go to *bed*." But I was a very disciplined student. Hardworking. I wanted to do well. And I got As.

But when I got really stressed-out, he'd put his foot down and say, "Let's call in sick and we can drive downtown and go out for lunch and then just get a copy of the test the next day."

I'd relent and say, "Oh, that's a great idea."

Then I'd cut school so we could drive along the lake to this spot on the west side where there were these swing sets and we would sit, swinging, talking, swinging some more, and have the best time. We'd go and get chili and crackers at this old-fashioned coffee shop. It just took the edge off. Or sometimes we'd just stay home and watch old movies. My dad admired strong female performers. He loved *Easter Parade* with Judy Garland and *National Velvet* with Elizabeth Taylor. He always wanted to hang out with me, and he loved it if I cut school.

My dad saw a picture in our local newspaper and showed everyone: "Look at this picture of Elizabeth Taylor in *National Velvet*. That looks like Molly!" He cut the picture out and saved it.

ONCE MARY AND I were both in high school, we started to do the typical teenage drinking at keg parties with our friends. Our dad figured teens are probably going to drink no matter what, so he didn't forbid it. He figured keeping an open line of communication was better than laying down the law. And that way if we ever did need his help for any reason, we could call him or talk to him.

He would always say, "Please, whatever you do, call me if you've had a couple of beers. I will happily come pick you up. But don't ever drink and drive. Please, girls! Never!"

And we listened. We were really good kids. We would drink a little, but we would never drive. Then he bought us Candie's high heels and $10,000 mink coats he got on discount, saying, "I want my girls to look glamorous and sophisticated in church. Doll yourselves up." My mink was two-tone.

I brought my Candie's to school and wore them with my uniform. One of the mothers who volunteered as a librarian just looked at me and shook her head and said, "Oh, your dad. Your dad *never* should have bought you those. Those are *prostitute* shoes."

I said, "Well, *Jim Shannon* thinks they're sexy and elegant."

Then my dad gave me my mom's old triple-shank diamond cluster ring to wear. I put on my Candie's and my mink and we went to a downtown gay bar called Traxx. I actually loved it. Mary liked it, too. He was off the wagon, and we were his show ponies. It felt like New York City. We drank beer and wore mink coats. And my dad would also party with my friends. One time he went to Traxx with Alison and me. She was all decked out in a long khaki trench coat, and after a while, as they got drunker and drunker, it just became a rowdy scene.

I said, "You guys are getting too wild! You guys are crazy. I'm going home and I'm going to *bed*."

My dad and Alison went on drinking until they decided to head to the bar next door. My dad tried to walk out with his drink but the bouncer stopped him. My dad got mad, poked the big bouncer in the chest in a kind of silly, Three Stooges way to make Alison laugh: "Listen, buster, don't tell *me* what I can and cannot do." They both walked to the bar next door and danced to the juke box. Then later my dad got his car, came back to the bar with the bouncer, and blocked the entrance so no one could get in or come out. Alison loved how bold he was. She got a kick out of his outrageousness. She was close to my dad. She would always say, "Your dad and me are two peas in a pod." Her father, a plastic surgeon, was quiet and intellectual. But when my dad wasn't drinking and acting crazy she could really talk to him.

MARY HEADED EAST TO attend Mount Vernon College in Washington, DC. When she came back to Cleveland for Christmas break, my dad and I picked her up from the airport. We wanted to hear each other's stories. But we *could not* tell our stories in the car. We had to wait until we'd sat down, ordered a glass of wine, ordered food. Only then could we begin our stories. It was a ritual. It was sweet. And with Mary away, my dad decided to do wild things with me all the time. He'd say, "How about if you cut school, call in sick, and we'll take a Mystery Trip?" And without even packing our bags, we would go to the airport and look at the boards in the main concourse: "There's San Francisco; there's Palm Beach. Let's go to Palm Beach, Florida!"

And we would get on the plane with no luggage, in the middle of a school day, pay on the plane with the credit card (People Express!), arrive in Palm Beach, and just stay at a hotel. We'd go to thrift shops for clothes. Mystery Trips!

I once cut school for a week, borrowed a bathing suit from

the woman who worked behind the desk at the Holiday Inn in West Palm Beach (it had really big cups), and wore it to the beach.

On Mystery Trips my father was the most fun to hang out with. On Mystery Trips he was like a fun brother/father.

But he could always flip. One time we went to Palm Beach, and when we got there he said, "This is costing me so much money and I didn't want to pay for it."

I said, "Then don't *offer* to pay for it."

He would tell me things that I shouldn't have known. Too private. Sexual stuff. Between a daughter and her single father, lines could be blurred. Like any family with codependency issues, sometimes you don't know what's appropriate or what isn't. Boundaries weren't defined. I was the person he relied upon emotionally. I think he needed my companionship.

Once, talking about a woman he was dating, he blurted out, "Oh God, I'm not good in bed. I come too fast."

I had no idea what to say. I just asked him, "Well, can't you slow down?"

Another time I read my dad a letter from a boyfriend that said, "I want to draw hieroglyphics on your body in sweat."

"Look, isn't that sweet?" I asked.

But my dad was so uncomfortable. I had taken it too far. He didn't like it at all. He was still my father. It crossed the line.

WHEN IT WAS TIME to apply to college, I went for a meeting at Hawken with this jock-type guy who for some reason was the college counselor. He was supposed to tell me what schools I should consider. But he was so unhelpful and discouraging.

I guess he didn't understand creative kids, or kids who

wanted to be in the arts, or girls. He just said, "Uh, maybe check out, like, Ohio State, or, you know, Ohio University." I remember feeling angry. I had really good grades. I wanted to go to school in New York City. But all he could suggest were schools in Ohio.

When I left that meeting, I was so mad that I took the big, thick college guidebook, the one with all the schools in it, and I *threw* it down the empty school hallway.

I thought, *I'm not going to listen to anything this guy says!*

My dad left the college application process up to me. So, on my own, I went through that big, thick college guide, found NYU's Tisch School of the Arts, and circled it. I thought, *I like this school. This drama school. New York University. This is where I want to go.*

My dad just said, "Okay. Apply. Do it."

NYU DID REGIONAL DRAMA auditions at a big hotel in Chicago, and applicants were expected to present monologues.

Monologues?

I didn't even know what a monologue was.

I went to the library and found a book called *Monologues for Teachers*. Stuff like "Good morning, boys and girls. My name is Mrs. Crimmons. And today we're going to be turning to page twenty-three in our textbooks."

I'm not sure this is going to be good, I thought. But I still checked out the book. That's how green I was.

I did eventually find some actual monologues, *really* dramatic ones—because I loved drama.

My dad, Mr. O'Neill, Alison, and I made a road trip out of my audition. It was so exciting. At this big Chicago hotel they were also holding Yale and Juilliard auditions. We saw all these high school kids practicing their monologues. They were nervous, pacing, talking to themselves, preparing for their big auditions. It was like in the movies. It was like *Fame*.

This is so cool, I thought. *These are the top drama students from all over the country, auditioning for Yale and Juilliard and NYU! Just this alone is so cool—to get here and see all this!*

My audition was for the head of the NYU Drama Department, Evangeline Morphos. I performed this dark, intense monologue from *Agnes of God*, where I had to scream, "Mommy! Mommy! Don't burn me!"

The button had fallen off my corduroys and I was holding them up with a safety pin, which popped open in the middle of my monologue and stuck me in the stomach. The pain added to the intensity.

And I knew I had done a good job. After my performance we sat and talked. She said, "What a great monologue. Well done." She was just very warm and kind.

And I got in!

When I saw that *big* envelope arrive at my house in Shaker Heights, Ohio, and I opened it and it said, "You have been accepted to New York University," I could not believe it. New York City, here I come! My dad and I went out to celebrate that night. We decided to go to an art house theater and see this movie about Andy Warhol's scene, *Ciao! Manhattan*, starring Edie Sedgwick. And I thought, *This is what my life is gonna be like in the Big Apple. Cool and artsy and creative!*

PART TWO

FREEDOM

CHAPTER 9

Drama School

I MOVED TO NEW YORK AND STARTED CLASSES AT NYU IN THE fall of 1984.

My dad and my sister Mary dropped me off. We were pulling up to Hayden Hall, my dorm, when all of a sudden two men came out of nowhere and, right in front of our car, one of them hit the other over the head with a baseball bat.

We screamed, and the man who got hit fell onto our windshield. Then a cop ran over and pointed his gun straight at our car.

My dad screamed, *"Duck!"*

A few minutes later, all of us shaking, my dad said, "Goodbye, Molly! Have a wonderful time at NYU!"

AFTER I WAS GONE, my dad was devastated. When Mary had left for college, he'd had a hard time, but he'd still had me at home. He'd relied on me even more. Now he was all alone. He missed me, and it was very heavy. He had lost his trusted companion. But I was ready for my own life and wanted to go, so he had to find other people to rely on. He had to learn how to let me go. I was ready to not be so dependent on him. He was not ready for that. I was ready to move toward a healthier place. He would have been happy to keep things the way they were.

It was hard for both of us.

AT COLLEGE I FELT like I was a divorcée. It was like *I'm free, yippee!* I felt as if I had gotten out of a crazy, long marriage, emotionally speaking. I just wanted to put on my character shoes and do monologues in Southern accents, saying, "Mama!"

And dating was not a priority; I was not ready to be involved. I had been my dad's primary companion for years, and the last thing I wanted to do now was have a boyfriend. Dating wasn't really something that I did in a serious way until much later. I had to really work on myself to have boyfriends and form normal relationships.

At the end of high school, just before I left for NYU, I'd met this boy named Tom Lux, who went to the public high school in Shaker Heights. He was really popular, really nice, and he was *cute*. He was also really into me. . . . I thought, *Oh, no. He thinks I'm one of those normal girls. But I've tricked him: he doesn't know that I'm a freak or that I'm scared. I appear normal but I'm not. He doesn't know my dark past.*

We went to a dance together and I was so nervous to get close to him while we were slow dancing. I wondered, *How do people get close and kiss and get together?* I had avoided that at all costs because I never wanted to get my heart shattered again. My thoughts went like this: *I ain't getting close to nobody. Not doing that. Not giving my heart to anybody. No way. No. Oh, no. I did that once with my mom when I was little and that did not lead to good things, so I am NOT doing that again.*

I could play along for a while, but then I knew: *I'm going to push you away. Because I think you think I'm normal and I'm not. I. Am. A. Freak.*

AT NYU I WENT from being at a small, private, preppie school where everybody knew everybody's story to this *big, diverse* university. My roommate was a girl in the nursing department. She was very bright and also a little nerdy. People said things about her like "Your roommate's *eccentric!* Some people think she's like a real witch."

But I thought, *I can do whatever I want. I can be friends with whoever I want. I'm going to be friends with the freaks and the geeks and I don't have to fit into any clique. And I'm free! And I like that witch. And I'm gonna be friends with that witch. And she and I are gonna go to the East Village for Chinese food on Sunday night. And we're gonna bring our own bottle of wine and sit and talk, that sweet, smart witch and I. And that is that.*

WHILE I WAS AT NYU, George Cheeks was at Yale. We used to take the train back and forth—New Haven to New York—to visit each other all the time. One time he came down and we ate fajitas at Panchito's, this Mexican place in the Village.

After we were done, I said, "We're both broke students. We really should dine and dash to save money."

George had never done anything like that. But he was game. "Let's do it!" he said.

So we did it, and the entire staff—manager, chef, cooks, waiters—chased us down the street. A mob of people came out and took off after us with pots and pans. They caught George first. I kept on running.

But he just said, "Oh, so sorry, did I not *pay*? Sorry!" and did such a good job pretending like he totally forgot that the whole thing blew over. After they left us alone, we were dying laughing—just in hysterics on MacDougal Street.

Then, when I visited him that first year at Yale, he asked me to pretend I was having sex with him. We slept in the same bed as friends. After we went into his room, I made these loud moaning sounds like we were really going at it. And when we came out in the morning, his suitemates high fived him as if to say, *Man, you got some!* It made George happy and I was thrilled to play along. But by the time he was a junior at Yale, he was dating a guy from Spain called Manolo.

WHEN I TURNED TWENTY that September, my dad visited and we went to the Oak Bar in the Plaza Hotel to celebrate. After the waiter came to our table, my dad ordered vodka neat with a glass of ice. He called that a "sidecar."

My dad liked the Oak Bar atmosphere, but it was really expensive—so the second the waiter turned his back, he drank down the vodka like a shot and refilled his glass with water really fast. I was so busy watching my dad refilling the glass, I wasn't able to see his face and how in the world he managed not to pucker his lips after drinking all that vodka.

Then my dad called the waiter back and said, "I just took a sip and this is watered down. I think it's *just water*!"

The surly waiter sniffed it suspiciously and brought more. But this time he came with the bottle so my dad could see him pour it. Stoli. Then we went to see *La Cage aux Folles* and after that to Don't Tell Mama for after-theater drinks.

The last time I'd seen him drinking, I'd asked him, "Why do you have to have a drink? Can't you have fun with just me? Aren't I enough?"

And he'd said, "It's not *that*. I just feel like I put on rose-colored glasses and I see the world in a nice pink glow, you know?"

And I'd thought, *Hmmm, I don't really get it, but all right.*

Now I just thought, *If you can't beat 'em, join 'em.*

I wasn't really in the mood to drink, but we partied the whole day. I could not keep up with my dad. I remember being so drunk that I went to the bathroom at some restaurant and passed out. I was a little lightweight.

As I lay on the floor, a woman came in and yelled, "*You!* Get up! Get out of here!"

I stumbled back into the bar and then we both got kicked out, physically, like bums, like in a cartoon: "You and your daughter get out of here!"

Then my dad pulled out his camera, taking pictures— *click, click, click, click*—and shouting, "I work for the *New York Times*! And I will *report* this establishment!"

The next time I went home, he showed me all these pictures of the staff hiding their faces.

AT NYU A LOT of students didn't have to work the way I did, and so they could take advantage of drama school by doing plays. I didn't have the time to even audition for anything, let alone rehearse if I got a part, because I was on financial aid and working thirty hours a week selling health club memberships and answering phones as a receptionist. I did that job for years. I could never even pick up a phone without automatically saying: "Park Avenue Squash and Fitness! This is Molly. Can I help you?"

I had to pull my own weight, so I worked at this health club and was a full-time college student. I went to all my classes, but I wasn't taking full advantage of NYU Tisch. (And obviously there was no time for dating in all this.)

I also worked in restaurants. I was the coat check girl at the Old Homestead Steakhouse, where all the waiters were professionals who'd been there for decades. Suki, the manager, wore bright red lipstick and black bell-bottom pants and spent her time in the kitchen counting cash. And the career waiters would always be sliding their fingers along this ledge up by the ceiling to get the drugs they'd hidden there. They'd dose up on Valium or whatever else before they started their shifts, to take the edge off.

I also started waiting tables at the Horn & Hardart Dine-O-Mat on the Upper East Side. It was a 1950s-nostalgia place with a jukebox where all the waitresses had to do little doo-wop and teeny-bopper performances. We would stop whatever we were doing and just do these memorized songs and dances. To make the time go faster, my coworkers and I bought really long fake ponytails and took on different personas. At the end of the night we'd sing songs from *Annie* and dream about a better life while we wiped down the tables to close up the shop.

But the second I heard the opening notes to Bobby Lewis's "Tossin' and Turnin'" I'd head down to the walk-in freezer and hide till the song was over. I would sit on the frozen turkeys and eat little orange slices. Nobody knew about my secret little hiding spot until one day I got caught by a manager.

One of the regular customers was this old guy, Elliott.

He said to me, "I wanna *help* you and be, like, your *manager*. Let me take you out to dinner and talk about it."

I didn't have any money. I thought, *Mmmm! He can be my sugar daddy.* So I let him take me out to Barbetta, one of the oldest Italian restaurants in the theater district. I ate all this delicious pasta. When the meal was over, he wanted me to hold his hand. I thought, *I'll hold his hand. Who cares? It's not that bad. It's worth holding his hand for this delicious spaghetti carbonara.*

After that, he took me out a bunch of times. He would show up at Horn & Hardart and tell people, "I'm her manager."

I WENT TO HIS apartment once. There were all these Irish girls living with him who wanted to be working actresses. But in the meantime I found out they were giving him blow jobs. He covered their rent and paid for their headshots, and they got a free place to live.

When I realized that, I felt so bad for the girls stuck there living with this creep, and I just thought, *He is disgusting.*

FRESHMAN YEAR I TOOK classes with a legendary drama teacher named Terry Hayden. She had a cane. She was tough. She'd tell students, "You're *gonna* make it. You're *never* gonna make it." People were scared of her. She could break you.

Terry taught sense memory, which was a popular acting technique. During what she called a "private moment" exercise in class, she asked students to get up and recall an emotional, personal experience from childhood. The exercise was designed to help actors feel they were in private while in a public space—to shed the self-consciousness that sometimes inhibits an actor's performance. For the exercise, we had to be very detailed and specific in reconstructing our memories, answering all sorts of questions for Terry. She gave us ten minutes to "experience the space" and then she asked us detailed questions.

"Where are you? How are you feeling? What do you smell? Do you see the oriental rug? What does it *feel* like to *touch* it?"

If you *were* really emotionally available, and if your "instrument" was free and ready, Terry would have you launch into performing whatever monologue you'd prepared, once she deemed you were in the right emotional place. If you were vulnerable and cried in front of the class when she went through her probing questions, it was like *Bravo*.

If you were bullshitting and pretending to be emotional and had walls up, Terry would call you out in this deadpan way, "No. Fake. You're *acting*. I don't believe it."

We all wanted her approval. It was like a therapy session.

One girl got up and did an exercise recalling her grandmother's funeral.

I thought, *Your grandmother's funeral? Ha! That's, like, nothing. Amateur hour.*

Oh, baby, I've got juicier material than this!

When it was my turn, Terry put me in front of the class and asked me about my parents and what life had been like when I was little. She was caring. She was careful. Her questions made me cry. I was open. I wasn't afraid. And it felt good to let it all out. She said, "Oh, my *darling, oh,* my *sweet girl*, if you can *access that*—and I see that you *can*—it's going to be *great*. You have so much to *pull* from!" After class, my fellow drama students came up and hugged me. They were very supportive and loving.

BUT THE MOMENT THAT really clicked for me was when we had to be clowns. Or Arlecchino, the comic relief from Italian commedia dell'arte plays. It was the final big project in this class taught by Alan Langdon, who ran NYU's professional acting program and was affiliated with Circle in the Square, a Broadway theater. We were supposed to research the subject on our own. Weeks and weeks of research! We also had to sew ourselves a fake penis to use as a prop and do a five-to-seven-minute routine. It's very acrobatic, too. Arlecchino needs to come out and entertain a whole huge theater, so whatever he does has to be *big* and *broad*. And always based around *lazzi*, the Italian word for slapstick gags, which are broken down into beats of three—meaning that if you fell down, you didn't just get back up, you did it again and again, always in threes. And this one performance would be our whole grade for the semester.

Other people in the class were renting out warehouse spaces to rehearse. I was like *Really? You're renting out a whole place to practice your Arlecchino?*

Oh, God, I thought. *I haven't practiced at all. What am I gonna do?* It was starting to make me *nervous.* But deep down in my heart I knew: *This is a big comic performance and I don't think it should be too rehearsed. It should be spontaneous and organic.*

When my performance day finally came, I had not rehearsed at all. The only thing I had done was sew my fake penis—which was fun.

I remember standing outside the door to the classroom before I began, heart pounding, no idea what I was going to do for the six minutes that were going to decide my whole grade for the semester. I was just scared *shitless.* But then I reminded myself, *It's okay that I don't have it all planned out.* I knew I would have to be brave and take chances as a performer.

When I stepped into the room to begin, I went crazy. I did my first *lazzo* trying to get through the door, succeeding the third time. The physical sequences can be improvised with exaggerated reactions, so I decided to spontaneously fall into the trash can that just happened to be in our theater classroom. Then of course it was very hard to get back *out* of that trash can. And naturally I waved that penis around! Then I pulled Alan, the teacher, into the scene to improvise with him. The students loved this—teasing the teacher and kind of giving him a hard time. In real life, he was *verrrry* serious, so I decided to kind of play with him, *as the character,* and the kids loved it. I could get away with it as Arlecchino. Kind of ribbing him: *Ooh, you think you're such a big deal, the big, tough acting teacher.* I was improvising *in character* but I used my *real* feelings, my suspiciousness of his know-it-all quality. And I just went completely wild. Something clicked and I went crazy improvising a big, wild comedic performance. The class was crying-laughing.

In the end I didn't just get a standing ovation. The whole class stood up on their chairs, cheering. It was a turning point in my life. With that Arlecchino I found myself as an artist and a performer. I learned I could make people really laugh. I learned to trust myself. That somewhere deep in my gut I *knew* not to over-rehearse but to just let it rip. Know the basic beats but then let yourself be free within those parameters, which is what I ended up doing years later on *SNL.*

DURING MY SEMESTER IN New York, I had a scene study partner named Gina Costello. She called me "Moll."

After we got paired up to do a scene together, we decided we'd meet to get to know each other. She asked if I could meet her at a hotel bar in Times Square.

At first I tried to protest, "Get to know each other and work on our scene in a Times Square bar? Seems kinda strange."

But she insisted and then slipped in "Well, I mean, maybe we can get some nice rich guy to buy us drinks or something. Come on, Moll."

I said, "I can lend you money if you need money." But then I said, "Okay," and just decided to go along with it.

We met at the bar and within five minutes we were getting free drinks from a Saudi sheik. He was flirting like crazy with Gina.

"You look like a princess," he told her.

After we'd downed a few free gin and tonics, I left to go to the ladies' room.

Gina followed after a few minutes. When she walked in, she was so excited, she could hardly speak.

"Moll, *Moll—guess what!*"

"What?"

"You're not going to believe this!"

"*What?*"

"Well, he said he knows we're students and he wants to help us out."

"Huh?"

She gave me this *Don't you get it?* stare: "*He. Knows. We're. Students. And. He. Wants. To. Help. Us. Out.*"

I didn't get it.

Gina lifted her eyebrows. "He wants us to come up to his *room*, Moll."

"*WHAT?!*"

"It won't take too long. Fifteen minutes is all. *Pleeease,* Moll."

"That's, like, *prostitution.*"

"Moll, *pleeease.* I want a new stereo set so badly."

"Gina, I just can't."

"Okay. I'll tell you what—how about you just come up to

the room with us? You don't have to do anything. I promise. Just come up and give me some support."

"Gina, if you want to go up there, I'll wait in the bar for you."

"What if something *happens to me*? Please, Moll, you've got to come up to the room."

She kept going on like this until I was feeling so guilty—and worried that if something happened to her it *would* be my fault—that I agreed to come up to the room.

We went back to the bar and then up to a suite on the twentieth floor. Gina told the guy that I was a virgin to keep him away from me. He was thrilled and he shouted, "You're a virgin!"

I was treasured goods.

But then he leaped on top of me, kissing ecstatically. He actually pushed me onto the bed so I was on my back. It wasn't violent or anything, but I could feel his weight on me till Gina hoisted him off and shouted, "No! No! Leave her alone! Don't touch her! She's a *virgin*! Get off of her!"

I was very, very innocent. We were tipsy. We did this silly striptease for him, bouncing on the bed and taking our tops off. I thought, *This is so weird and crazy.* I kept reminding myself, *This is a wild city you've chosen to live in, Molly. New York City. Crazy adventures. Stuff like this happens.* But then *he* started taking his clothes off. He had this potbelly. I ran into the bathroom and put on my top. When I came back out Gina was giving him a blow job.

He was in ecstasy.

I thought, *I'm a Catholic girl. Gina is a naughty girl.* She did not seem concerned with my presence at all. She seemed like a professional. I went back into the bathroom. After a few minutes she came in, too.

I told her, "I'm sorry but I've got to get out of here."

She said, "Just give me five more minutes. Five minutes. Just five minutes. That's *it*. I promise. Then we'll go."

"*Five* minutes. All right."

I twiddled my fingers in the bathroom for a while. But when the sheik began moaning in pleasure I walked back into the room. Gina looked up from underneath him, gave me a little friendly wave, and held up three fingers to indicate how much longer it was going to take. The sheik didn't notice that I was in the room again because his back was to me. I wasn't even really fazed. I started putting on my coat. *Come on, let's get out of here,* I signaled to her, waving my hands. *Let's wrap this up.*

Enough was enough.

Gina shook her head and mouthed, *Check his wallet! Check his wallet! Check his wallet!*

I quickly went through his clothes. I'd never done that before. It felt wrong, but I wanted to get out of there fast. In the end, all I could find in his pockets was a five-dollar bill and a ten-dollar bill. So I grabbed some hotel stationery and wrote in big block capitals, "JUST A 5 AND A 10, LET'S *GO!*" and held the piece of paper up so she could read it from across the room.

She took the hint and got out from under him.

He ended up having a secret stash of cash somewhere in the closet and giving us $600 each from a big wad.

We took a cab home in the pouring rain and she was mad that we'd been given equal shares.

"I can't believe we both got the same amount! I had to do all the dirty work! You didn't even do anything!"

She wanted some of my half but eventually relented.

"Then you have to pay for the cab ride home, Moll. It's

only fair. I'm going to take my boyfriend out to celebrate," she said.

I felt numb. I felt dirty. But I was fine paying for the cab.

"You're going to tell your boyfriend about tonight?" I asked.

"Oh, yeah, he'll get a kick out of it."

"I don't think he'll think it's very funny."

The driver let Gina off first and then he started flirting with me.

ABOUT TWO DAYS LATER, another very good NYU drama school friend, Ruby, called me up and said, "You are not going to believe what just happened to me last night."

Immediately I knew.

"Oh, I bet I *can* believe it," I said.

Ruby was a super-serious, brilliant actress. She told me she'd wound up trapped in a hotel bathroom reading *Man and Superman* for her theater history class. This time Gina told her trick that Ruby was her personal bodyguard. When he refused to pay her, she ran into the bathroom and asked Ruby to run back out there and get her clothes. To keep her distance, Ruby scooped up Gina's clothes with the tip of an umbrella, like Mary Poppins. Then Gina made Ruby go back out there and say, "We want cab fare home." And then he said, "I ain't giving you nothing."

Gina was eighteen that night in Times Square. I think about her from time to time and I hope she's doing well.

CHAPTER 10

The Birth of Mary Katherine Gallagher

FOR YEARS MY DAD HAD BEEN GIVING ME ALL SORTS OF career advice, saying things like "Put on your high heels. Doll yourself up. And you march right into the offices of those Hollywood agents and say, 'Hey, hold the phone—I got *talent*!' And don't forget: Use your singing voice."

So, when I got a meeting in New York City with Barbara Jarrett, a talent manager who represented a ton of child actors, I *did* sing. I walked in, hopped up on her desk, and launched into the song "Chicago"—the Judy Garland version, in honor of my father: "Chicago, Chicago, that toddling town, that toddling town!"

I was belting it out. And Barbara started clicking her fingers!

Then she said, "You *got it*, kid!"

And I was signed.

BARBARA JARRETT REPRESENTED ANOTHER actress my age who was getting a lot of calls because she had full-color headshots.

They were a lot more expensive than the black-and-white ones. But headshots were your calling card, and I thought, *Ooooh, I want to do full-color headshots. Everybody has black-and-white. Color's going to get attention.*

So this other actress sent me to the guy who did hers, this trendy fashion photographer. Headshot photography was big business. I gave him all my money from working at the health club. Then, on the day of the shoot, I got my makeup and hair done. (As part of the package headshot fee, someone would do your hair and makeup.) I was feeling so pretty and excited.

The photographer studied me while his model girlfriend stood behind him.

I thought, *I'm going to take over this town.* I felt like a million bucks.

Then he asked me, "Why are you *so ugly?*"

The model girlfriend, giggling, said, "Oh my God, cut it out!"

What a jerk.

"Why are you so ugly?"

But I was devastated.

BARBARA JARRETT GOT ME some work on soap operas. But I also started to think, *Gosh, here I am at NYU, paying all of this money. I really need to take advantage of college.* There were kids who had everything paid for by their parents who were constantly onstage and being seen. I thought, *I'm gonna audition for one of the school productions.* Another NYU drama student also worked at Park Avenue Squash and Fitness selling memberships. His name was Eugene Pack and he is now an Emmy-nominated and Drama Desk Award–winning writer-producer-performer. He cast me as Mona May in the

NYU staging of *Come Back to the 5 & Dime Jimmy Dean, Jimmy Dean,* the dramedy Robert Altman used as the basis for the movie that fascinated Ann and me when we were girls. Eugene directed the production, too.

THEN, IN MY LAST year, I tried out for this on-campus comedy revue show called *The Follies,* where students would make fun of all the teachers. We did the show in a black-box theater at midnight. And there were great writers working on it: David Weincek and Michael Sayers. Dan Jinks produced. Madeleine Olnek was the writer-director.

This was the first time I ever tried out for something comic—and I got cast. It was a very small cast. And Adam Sandler got cast as well. He was unknown to the public but at NYU he was already famous. He would do stand-up shows in the cafeteria at Weinstein, the dorm where he lived—just get up and do a set. And people loved him. He was quickly becoming *very* well-known on campus. Students were like "Oh my God—*Sandler*!" And he was the one student who was hustling at night (other than Gina!). Working his act out at stand-up clubs. Honing his material. He was probably working harder than anyone in that entire drama school. Most people were just studying acting. But Adam was so ambitious and focused, and onstage all the time when he was really still a kid. You could see at a very young age that he was a standout.

But Madeleine thought he was shy, so she asked me, "Could you take Adam out for coffee? So you can maybe bring him out of his shell."

I just said, "Adam Sandler is *not* shy. And I do not think Adam Sandler needs *my* help. It's gonna be the reverse—I'm gonna need Adam's help."

But obviously Madeleine had good taste.

During rehearsal one day we did an improv exercise where she was a big movie director who was very hard to please, and we had to try to win her over to get a part.

"Don't think about it too much," she said. "Just make up a character and walk through the door and introduce yourself and try to impress me."

I just walked in and without any time to plan—on total impulse—blurted out, "Hi. I'm Mary Katherine Gallagher!"

I was doing the character as a very nervous person—just an exaggerated version of myself and kind of how I felt.

And when Madeleine was *not impressed* I'd have to come back and try to impress her more. I loved how I could pull from myself and create. By helping me find this character inside myself, Madeleine was like the midwife for Mary Katherine Gallagher.

It was a whole new world of writing a character and then working with this great team shaping the show. Not only did they put me in *The Follies* but they ended up creating a second whole show around this early version of the Mary Katherine Gallagher character. This first version of the character wore red pants and a red shirt and turned out to be a murderess. The midnight performances got so raucous and the show was so popular that there were lines around the block to get in. The show and Mary Katherine Gallagher became an on-campus hit. Students would recognize me and say to each other, "Oh my God, it's that girl!"

Before doing *The Follies* I was a very serious dramatic actress. But then people started saying, "You should be on *Saturday Night Live!*"

I thought, *Really?* I'd never considered that before.

I realized, *God, comedy comes so naturally for me.* It was a real revelation, people saying, "You should do comedy." It was fantastic. I loved it. It just felt so right. So this show was another major turning point in my life.

For the whole summer after the Mary Katherine Gallagher debut I kept getting congratulated. After a while the praise began to have its effect: *Maybe I should go to LA and try to get on TV and pursue this comedy thing,* I thought.

Huh, comedy.

I HAD GONE OUT to LA in the summer of 1987, before my last year of NYU. I wanted to see if I liked California. And I thought maybe I could get an agent out there. I lived at the USC dorms because they were dirt cheap, $15 a week. But USC was on the east side of LA, far from everything. I didn't know anybody, I didn't have a car, and I was very lonely. To survive, I got a job as a waitress at the Old Spaghetti Factory on Sunset Boulevard. I had to take the bus to work, seven miles away.

The Old Spaghetti Factory was a giant, disgusting restaurant. They had a rodent problem and told me to "keep it low key" if I saw anything scurrying around.

One night, as I was carrying a massive tray of spaghetti to some customers, a rat crawled across the floor in front of me and I leaped up on a chair in the center of the packed dining room and started pointing and screaming, "Ewwww! Gross! A rat! A rat! Look!" I pointed it out to everyone. I created such a scene. People ran out of the restaurant. A little baby threw up. Then I slipped off the chair and spaghetti flew everywhere.

One of the managers said, "Please, don't ever make a scene like that again."

I mostly worked at night. Before the customers arrived, we had to practice our serving skills by waiting on the managers, and they would quiz us on the menu. Then I carried huge trays of pasta classics and these oversized jugs of wine and got as fit as I could get because the place was so big and I was always zipping back and forth, carrying so much weight. I got very thin that summer running all around that giant restaurant.

I met some other actors from the USC drama program hanging out by the dorm pool. They were always just swimming and laughing and having barbecues and taking ecstasy on weekends. There were visiting professors in the dorm, too, and I met a scientist in his early fifties who looked like Max von Sydow's character in *Hannah and Her Sisters*.

He asked if I wanted to have coffee one day and I was so lonely I responded, really enthusiastically, "*Please*, let's have coffee!" We went to the Sizzler. He talked about science, and I was delighted. He was really sweet. He kept me company for a while, just as a friend.

I felt very anxious around the USC drama students. They were always *relaxing* and *chilling by the pool*. A part of me wished I could be more like them, but then another part thought, *Gosh, they're so lazy. How can they just hang out by the pool midday? There's so much work to be done! Shouldn't we all be passing out our headshots, taking advantage of our youth? We're young! Let's get these faces out there!*

I put my headshots in a bag and took the bus to Samuel French, a theatrical bookstore, where you could buy plays and scripts and books about the acting business. I bought a paperback with agents' addresses in it and then I would walk up and down Sunset Boulevard, slipping my picture under their doors.

Then I would come home and swim and eat baked potatoes with a side of vegetables for dinner in my furnished dorm room. Eventually, I got lonely enough I called my dad, who was so excited that I needed him that he came out for a visit.

"I'll be right there!" he said.

He stayed with me for a week and rented a car so he could drop me off and pick me up from my shifts. I'd get in the car and count the money I had made—like, $45—and he'd just say, "Yeah, that's how you learn, you know: you gotta make your dollar and know the value of a buck and that's the way it goes." I understood what he was trying to teach me.

But a part of me wished that I could have been more like my barbecuing and partying neighbors. I felt like I was too rigid, so one night I went out with them. But after a few hours keeping up with them, I felt exhausted. I had to go to the bathroom, so this pair of girls I didn't know said, "Let's make a choo-choo train," and we all went together, putting our hands on each other's hips. They were very sweet. *Chuga-chugachugachuga choo-choo!* To the bathroom. And I felt this drunk love for them.

But they did that all summer long, all the time. I partied with them once and thought, *I am never doing this again.* I felt so dehydrated the next day. I wasn't willing to waste that kind of time. None of those people ended up making it.

ONE AFTERNOON, as I was going from building to building through the Beverly Hills part of Sunset, delivering my headshots, Gary Coleman's agent, Mark Randall, opened his door and invited me to come in. He was tall and very tan, dressed California casual.

It was a large office with little teddy bears and other stuffed animals strewn around it. The only photograph in the office was a gigantic portrait of Gary Coleman. Mark just happened to be there and "took a meeting" with me on the spot.

He said, "Take a little spin. Let me see you."

I did a spin for him. I was so naive.

Then he said, "Now sit down and tell me about yourself!"

I was *dying*! To me this was Big Time.

He said, "I really want to help you. I'm going to introduce you to my friend" who is a big soap opera casting director.

I thought, *Oh my God! This is so exciting!*

Gary Coleman had just gotten off *Diff'rent Strokes* and was a big star. I was over the moon. *If he signs me,* I thought, *his clients will be me and Gary Coleman! I'll have a talent agent who represents Gary Coleman.*

Mark said he would pay for new headshots, which was a huge deal, because they were *expensive.* Then he invited me up to his big, fancy house in the hills in Los Feliz. A lot of girls seemed to live there with him. They all walked around in bikinis. He suggested *I* put on my bathing suit and get in his hot tub for my big headshot photo shoot—which I did. It was ridiculous. Me, in a hot tub, in a bathing suit. I still have the headshots somewhere.

His house was huge—with a pool, a Jacuzzi, and an unbelievable view.

Mark suggested we do some scenes together so I could practice my acting. He got out a script and we read together.

Then, as part of one sexy scene, he reached over and started to unbutton my shirt. Coming from NYU drama school, being a very serious actress, *into taking risks,* I was up for anything. So I thought, *Yeah, yeah, yeah, go for it! Go ahead! Unbutton it!*

I really wanted to commit to the role.

It was like he was testing me to see how far he could take it. But then, all of a sudden, it seemed sleazy. I had to stop him.

He played it cool, said, "Okay," and didn't push it any further.

THE ONLY "WORK" MARK ever got me that summer was modeling for a hair show in Marina del Rey. He drove all the live-in actresses and me to a salon in Beverly Hills, where a Japanese hairdresser made my hair into what looked like a tidal wave. The actual show was a blur. I strutted down the runway and modeled my wave. When it was over, Mark took the girls and me out to the Cheesecake Factory in Marina del Rey to celebrate. I made a hundred bucks.

BUT A FEW WEEKS LATER, in the fall of 1987, when I was back at school, I got a call from Mark. He said he was coming to New York City with Gary Coleman and asked if I wanted to meet them for tea at the Plaza Hotel. I was over the moon. *Meeting my West Coast agent at the Plaza Hotel. La-di-da!*

When I arrived, Gary stood up like a gentleman and Mark sat me next to him. After pushing in my chair, Gary held my hand. He was eighteen years old but so little. I thought he was cute as a button. He was all dressed up in an expensive suit.

He was also very flirtatious with me throughout the tea, saying, "You remind me of Kimberly from *Diff'rent Strokes*."

I was flying—*flying*—with excitement. It was the biggest compliment. I *loved* Dana Plato. She was so cute and bubbly. I couldn't believe that I reminded Gary of his co-star. I was thinking, *That means I can make it in Hollywood. Maybe I'll be on the next* Diff'rent Strokes. *If only I could be in her position. . . .*

We had a great time, laughing and joking. Then they asked me if I wanted to come up and see Gary's suite—which was the Presidential Suite, on the top floor.

I said, "Sure!"

Gary held my hand on the elevator.

The suite was *H-U-G-E*. Gary showed me around, and when we got to his room he closed the door and said, "Sit on my bed."

I sat on his bed.

From there I had a view of his kidney dialysis machine in the corner.

He hopped up on the bed next to me. The possibility of something sexual occurring hadn't even crossed my mind. I was an innocent virgin still. (*Still*. And I had just turned twenty-two.) He was playful at first, tickling me, trying to lie on top of me and smooch me. Then, when I pushed him away and stood up, Gary climbed up on the bed and jumped off, using it as a springboard to launch himself onto me, kissing me wildly and sticking his hands under my shirt.

But he was so *little*, I was able to just flip him back off onto the floor. It wasn't very hard.

He bounced right back onto the bed and wrapped himself around me again. Bed jumping was clearly a technique for him.

"Whoa," I said. "*Hey!* Come on. *Come on!*" And I flipped him back off onto the floor.

He got back up and came at me again.

I shouted, "Come *on*, Gary, knock it off. I don't even know you." I was laughing nervously.

When he started kissing my neck, I told him, "Okay, this is not funny, *Gary!*" I threw him off again.

This happened multiple times. I would *throw* him across

the room and he'd use the bed to bounce right back on top of me. He kept bouncing back and I kept flipping him off. It was exhausting. He would not give up.

Finally, I started to walk away and he changed strategies. He *crawled* back over, grabbing my ankle, wrapped his whole upper body around my calf, and then I was *dragging* him across the floor. As I walked, he held on tight.

"No, Gary!" I shouted. This time I had to *shake* him off my leg—hard.

Then I ran across the room and locked myself in the bathroom, out of breath.

He followed, got down on the floor, stuck his hand under the door, waved his fingers, and said, *"I can seeeee you, Silly Billy!"*

What am I going to do? I wondered.

My hair was all messy.

I wanted to be on the next *Diff'rent Strokes* . . . but this was *disturbing.* And sad. And so awkward. With his dialysis machine out there in the hotel room.

Gary's relentlessness was unlike anything I've ever experienced. While he was in the middle of this attack, I both couldn't believe what was happening to me and couldn't wait to tell my friends. I was already thinking about *how* I was going to tell them. I was turning it into a story as it was happening, but I was also genuinely shocked. Obviously, he assumed that I wanted to fool around because I came up to the hotel room—but he was so aggressive, it was crazy.

I didn't run out until he stopped trying to get in. I waited till he gave up. And he was so little, I didn't feel physically in danger. It didn't seem that threatening—more kooky than anything else.

Then I dashed out fast, blurting, "I gotta go!" Once I made

it out the door, Gary straightened up and acted like nothing had ever happened. I went out into the hallway and back down on the elevator and found Mark in the restaurant near the lobby. Unfortunately, I didn't say anything that strong to him.

I just told him, "That client of yours is *wild*. You gotta keep a *lid* on him. You have to *watch* that client of yours."

I didn't say anything more. I never heard from Mark Randall after that. I told this whole story on *Conan* in the late 1990s, while Gary was still very much alive. He never contacted or contradicted me. He knew what had happened.

CHAPTER 11

The Mamet Scam

WHEN I WAS AT NYU DRAMA SCHOOL, YOU REALLY weren't supposed to audition for anything outside of the drama program. They wanted their students to focus on their training. But I wanted to be a pro! I knew I was ready! So I auditioned on the side, doing very dark, dramatic *Oh, Mommy, don't burn me! Please don't burn me!* kinds of monologues.

The casting directors on a soap called *Another World* were thrilled: "We want you on the show!" they told me, so I got my first "under five"—the industry term for a role with less than five lines. This was promising, and I immediately bought into SAG.

Now I was eligible for union jobs and dental care!

I graduated from NYU in 1987 and stayed in New York for a year after that, trying to get more stuff cooking. My thinking was I'd give New York City a year and see if something happened and then I'd try LA.

I MADE A FAKE Actors' Equity card that I used to sneak into professional Broadway auditions. One time I made it really far on my fake Equity card, down to the callbacks for this big Broadway musical called *Smile*, about teen beauty pageants. There had been an open call, which meant *hundreds* of people came in, and they narrowed it down to the final twenty. Debbie Allen was slated to be the choreographer. And they told us, "You have to be able to sing and move well."

Even though I wasn't a professional dancer, they wanted singers who could learn a basic dance routine, and I made it to the final twenty.

And for the next callback, Debbie Allen was there with all the producers, a table of ten people.

She said to me, "Okay, well, you made it this far! So now let's see your moves. What do you got for us?"

Show her my moves, I thought. *Just make up any dance? Just agile-freestyle. I just have to dance. With no music.*

Yes. And I had to do it for a full minute. I did some spins, clicked my fingers, did a little chassé, some leaps, threw in a little robot dance, and then my big finish: freezing like a statue with jazz hands. They were not impressed. It was the worst. I did not get the part.

I BOUGHT A CHEAP belted blue-and-white dress at Bolton's and wore it uptown to slide my headshots under the doors at agencies in this big building on West Fifty-Seventh Street. Then I took the bus back downtown and hoped someone would call me—at my service's number. I paid ten bucks a month to this company where actual women at a switchboard would take down messages so you wouldn't miss out if someone was calling with a job for you—real old-timey. I would call in to see if I had any messages. And there was nothing sadder than hearing "Nope. No messages."

But one agency did call me in for an interview. I wore my Bolton's dress while an assistant videotaped me and asked me questions. Then the head of the agency watched the tape to see what I looked like on camera. As she studied me on the recording, she lit up a cigarette. She was just silently watching the video as she smoked. I sat there, too, and we watched the video together. While she took drags on her cigarette and let out the smoke, she kept shaking her head *No*. I went from being really excited to riding a bus home in my cheap Bolton's dress with her cigarette smoke clinging to it. Frozen. Staring out the window. Heart sinking. Replaying the whole scene in my head. Just feeling like the pits. Thinking, *This is awful.*

I GOT A REAL job as a booker for runway models at a big-time modeling agency. I figured, since I had my NYU degree, I should get a serious nine-to-five job. My boss—the main booker guy—would send me out into the lobby on Friday afternoons to check over models' lookbooks for our open calls. I had no idea what I was doing.

I'd say things like "This shot of you is stunning!" As if I were some professional. But I just felt bad for the models.

THEN MY FRIEND EUGENE Pack and I decided to move out to LA together to do our own shows and try to get on television. I did not want to go to LA by myself. I had done that the summer before and been so lonely. I knew if I went back to LA, I was going to go with a friend, so the two of us headed out west together. We sublet an apartment from someone Eugene knew in the Villa Elaine, right across from the El Pollo Loco on Fountain and Vine, in Hollywood. Our first two months in Hollywood were vacation months. We went swimming every single day under the palm trees and ate out all the time. Then we buckled down and started buying copies of *Drama Logue* every week to look for open-call auditions.

I took out multiple cash advances on my credit card and rented a wreck. Eugene rented a wreck, too.

My dad said, "That's life, it's tough, figure it out."

But after a while he changed his mind and said, "I could buy you a car."

I wanted a car, but I knew not to accept. Because I knew that in some moment when he was in a bad mood about something he'd turn it around and guilt me and say, "I *paid* for that car. That cost a lot of money." I wasn't falling into that trap. But I also think it was good of him to not just tell me, "Oh, Molly, here's a check." It kept me hungry. (Literally.) I learned how to rely on myself. It's good when you're worried about paying your rent and you have to figure it out or work more or take more shifts or save or not spend as much. My dad wanted me to learn this and I did.

EUGENE MET A WOMAN who worked as a headhunter for big talent agencies and movie studios—William Morris, Creative Artists Agency, International Creative Management. And that was a big break. She liked us because we were smart NYU graduates and she would send us out all over Los Angeles. We'd be up in the morning drinking our coffee and get a call.

"Hey, Molly, can you go answer phones today?"

And I would put on my skirt and my nice blouse and head over to CAA. I would buy business-looking clothes at thrift shops to look "office professional."

I was temping for the head of Warner Bros. when Goldie Hawn came in. She looked so pretty and young. And what was so interesting was that I could tell by the way she was looking in the mirror before the meeting that she was really nervous and had made a big effort to look sexy for the studio head. She was really working it. I just thought, *What is she so worried about? She's Goldie Hawn.*

CAA was in a high-rise on Avenue of the Stars in Century City.

For my lunch break, I went to a little windowless coffee shop in the basement—this dumpy place with sandwiches and a couple of four tops.

One time a guy came in and I thought, *I know him.* We exchanged glances.

Then I realized, *Oh my God, it's Charlie Sheen!*

He had a production company at Orion in the same building. He walked up to my table and said, "Mind if I join you?"

I thought, *No problem, Charlie.*

He sat down and was *so* nice.

He totally opened up to me. "Becoming a semi-star was really overwhelming. I started drinking a lot during *Wall Street* because I couldn't deal with the girls and the exposure," he said.

"That sounds hard," I said.

"Yeah," he said. "I lost control. But now I'm down to two beers a day."

"Oh, that's good," I told him.

I thought, *Charlie is so down-to-earth.*

EUGENE WOULD TELL ME hilarious stories about this one big agent who made him go to the Cheesecake Factory and pick up her chocolate chip cheesecakes. Then he'd hear her talking on the phone, saying, "Why am I so fucking fat? I'm a fat hog."

That agent repped a hot up-and-coming actress who would come around on her way to Vegas and drop off these slobbering St. Bernards for Eugene to walk all around Beverly Hills.

One of the big agencies started to hire me a lot because I was personable.

They put me on the desks of two big agents. One would never ask me to do anything. He'd just smile and say, "Hey, Molly, ya good?" Now he cracks up that I was his temp.

The other had two full-time assistants and one of them asked me, "Do you know how to roll calls?"

I wasn't sure what she was talking about, but I had the general idea, so I said, "Yeah, sure. I know how to roll calls."

"He's going to return calls after lunch and you gotta just keep the calls rolling. You know, you just get 'em on the line? And keep 'em rolling?"

"Sure, yeah, I can do that," I said.

She sent me into his huge, snazzy office. The agent had a little foam basketball and he was bouncing it against a wall, with a headset on. Since he had about thirty calls to return, he had to do a new call every four minutes to get through them all in a couple hours. My job was to have five waiting on hold while he talked, lights blinking, so he could move quickly to the next call—bounce and roll, bounce and roll, bounce and roll. At the time, he represented Sarah Jessica Parker and Robert Downey Jr., who happened to be dating.

I sat off to the side, with him not even looking at me. When Sarah Jessica Parker came on the line, I passed the call over and he said, "*Hey, S.J.!* What's going on?"

My mom

Me as a baby

My dad and mom on a date, before they had kids

St. Dominic's school photo, with pixie haircut

This was an era when people dressed up to go to the airport. My mom was always so well dressed, and she dressed the three of us up, too. From left to right, my little sister, Katie, me, and my big sister, Mary.

My dad cleaning the dining room chandelier

Playing house with Ann Ranft, 1975

Photo taken shortly after the car accident. The photographer was trying to make me smile—he even came up and tickled my face with a feather—but I felt so sad.

My sister Mary and I on a trip to California

In California

With Ann Ranft, when we were in high school

Studying in my den, wearing my St. Dominic's uniform

George Cheeks and I in *The Wizard of Oz* at the Heights Youth Theater

My dad and Mr. O'Neill

Photo taken by my friend John
MacInnis when we were at Tisch

Shortly after graduating from NYU, my friend Addie Tavormina and I went up to the roof of our apartment on West 57th Street and took this photo.

With Eugene Pack, when we were struggling actors

Goofing around with Marie in front of Cravings after work

With Alison Earle, 1990

With Debra and Mike Palermo, Thanksgiving, 1991

The cast of *Saturday Night Live* during the 1997–1998 season. *Credit: @ediebaskin*

A 1997 cover of *Rolling Stone*, shot by Mark Seliger

My first-ever Mary Katherine Gallagher sketch, in 1995, with Gabriel Byrne blocking my white underwear. *Credit: @ediebaskin*

"And Father I can do gymnastics . . . backflip!" *Credit: @ediebaskin*

Doing my character, Helen Madden, Licensed Joyologist. "I love it, I love it, I love it!" *Credit: @ediebaskin*

Doing our sketch "NPR's: Delicious Dish: Schweddy Balls" with Alec Baldwin and Ana Gasteyer. *Credit: @ediebaskin*

Behind the scenes at *SNL*, getting notes from the writers Paula Pell and Scott Wainio. *Credit: @ediebaskin*

Backstage at *SNL*, getting ready to do my character Sally O'Malley

As Sally O'Malley, with Christopher Walken. *Credit: @ediebaskin*

With my dad in Washington, DC, for the second Clinton inauguration, 1997

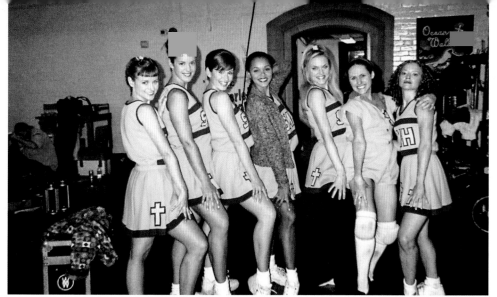

During the shooting of *Superstar: The Movie*, directed by Bruce McCulloch

My dad goofing around while visiting me on the set of *Superstar* in Toronto

With Lorne Michaels and my dad on the set of *Superstar*

At the premiere of *Superstar* with Steven Levy, my manager, and George Cheeks

Dear Molly,

To the most wonderful daughter a Father could ask for that's you! Thoughtful, considerate, kind, loving, always putting your best foot forward.

Accomplished, successful talented, hard worker, excellent sense of humor – a true delight to be around. You make people smile and laugh even when they don't want – That's Molly Shannon – Wishing you the best your ever. good health, joy love. peace & MUCH happiness. All my love always – Daddy,

Buy yourself a dress & use part of this check to really get what you want Have a wonderful Birthday –

September 16, 2001

↑

this is Right after our LA/OJAI CALIFORNIA TRIP XO♡

With warm thoughts of you,
today and always.

A letter my dad wrote me right after he came out to me in California

My dad and I getting ready in Hair and Makeup for the *SNL* Mother's Day special, as I was leaving the show in 2001

With Stella as a newborn

With my kids, Stella and Nolan, in our New York City apartment, 2005

Nolan and Stella in New York City

With Stella and Nolan in San Francisco

With Fritz and the kids in Los Angeles

I was thinking, *This is so great. He's actually talking to Sarah Jessica Parker from* Square Pegs. *This is so cool.*

Then she put him on with Robert Downey Jr.

"Downey, how you doing, man? Cool, cool, cool!"

All while shooting some hoops with his little basketball.

He would do a little quick business in all these calls. "So, yeah, hey, they want to do a remake of this show from Denmark. I'm going to send you the script. . . ."

And I'm hearing what he's saying and thinking to myself, *I'm a spy. This is what these people do. Wow, how the hell do you get up to this level? This. Shit. Is. Fascinating.*

But then he's giving me signals, circling his index finger, like *Keep the calls rolling, keep it going, keep it going! Faster, faster!*

But I wasn't fast enough. *I. Wasn't. Fast. Enough!* Suddenly, I didn't have them lined up. I had nobody for him. I was in the middle of scrambling to get somebody when he literally kicked me out and hauled another assistant in mid-call.

I was sent home.

RIGHT AFTER THAT, an actor acquaintance from NYU got a part as a cashier on the sitcom *Growing Pains*.

And I was jealous. He had only been in LA for a few weeks. I thought, *I wish I could get a job like that! He got a guest spot on a series.* And even though it was so ridiculous that it was *Growing Pains*, I just couldn't get over it.

How come he gets a part on Growing Pains *and I get nothing? Why, God, why? It's just not fair!*

Then my dad told me, "Remember, you can always come home anytime. I'll send you the money and the ticket."

I was temping, I was broke, and I just thought, *This is so hard.* I went out for a walk and cried, talking to God: "It's taking *forever*! I'm *still* really struggling! It's. Just. Not. *Fair!*"

But during that walk suddenly I had an epiphany. I thought, *At least I'm out here doing what I love, pursuing what I love, trying.* So many people I'd gone to college with had given up on their dreams. And a lot of people from my high school had moved back to Ohio after college and weren't really pursuing what they wanted. I thought to myself, *At least I'm in LA, doing what I want. That alone is a very meaningful life. That's actually a good, brave thing.* I thought, *You're doing more than most people will ever do. I don't care if I keep trying till I'm sixty. I'm gonna try till I'm a grandmother. And I'm just gonna enjoy the process. Yes, it's hard, but at least I'm out here doing what I want. That's a very good thing that most people aren't even brave enough to do.*

NOW, THIRTY YEARS LATER, that's still my spiritual/business philosophy. Struggle itself is meaningful. You never know where anything is going to go. You don't know. I didn't know if I would ever make it. But I have a positive attitude and I think people always see that in me. And I still pursue show business that same way.

Now, decades later, what I would tell actors struggling, auditioning for a part, would be: *Don't worry so much about getting some part. You never know what they're looking for, so don't take it so personally. Don't look at it like* I've really got to get this part. *Just look at it as a meeting. When I go for an audition, I try not to be result oriented.*

Maybe you're not right for this part but they'll remember you later for something else. You never know. Just think,

Hey, I get to meet this person. Look at it as laying down your groundwork. Building your relationships. Maintaining your relationships. Hollywood is so small, it's like a high school. The town can seem so overwhelming at first. Geographically it's giant and spread out. But people are all connected. Everybody knows everybody. You always have to hustle no matter what level you're at, so you might as well enjoy where you are and not compare.

I've seen people who are superstar movie stars who still feel like they are only as good as their last movie, and they are full of fear and insecurity. And I think, *Wait a minute,* you *are scared? Well, in that case, I better just enjoy where I am, because if* you're *scared, then we are all fucked.*

And then it's important to go to the people who love you and who *want* to work with you as opposed to trying to convince people who don't. If there's some obstacle, maybe there's a reason for it. I always look at stuff that way. No matter how far you've come, what level of success you've achieved, you're always going to have to get to the next place, so you might as well enjoy where you *are.* Be creative and enjoy your work. Just enjoy the process.

I try not to buy in to the feeling that I don't measure up. To me, that's an old childhood pattern. Hollywood can sometimes make you feel like you're never enough, with its ups and downs. But I try hard to enjoy life . . . on earth . . . as an artist. It makes me feel good when people come up to me and say, "You make me so happy. You make us laugh." That's what it's all about. Making people feel good. It's not about *yourself.* I like to think about what movies and storytelling do for people. And how you can make people forget their troubles. I like the extension of myself. You can show an audience how a character is feeling—they are with you—and then maybe they can understand a part of themselves through the character or performance.

In 2003, I did this TV series called *Cracking Up*. It was created by my good friend, the dazzling Mike White, a writer/director/performer I worship. But the network didn't get behind the show: they kept trying to get Mike to change it, and it was not a good experience for him. We shot thirteen episodes and only two aired. But Mike and I became really good friends. We'd have dinners and he'd say, "I'm gonna write you a movie."

And I'd think, *You are? That would be great!*

I was so excited, but I also didn't want to ask him about it or bother him too much, because I knew how hard he worked and I knew that the whole experience on *Cracking Up* was really difficult. So I thought, *If he does this, it should just be creative and no pressure and he should just have fun writing.* And then one day he called me up and said, "I have a script to send you." And it was like a dream come true—a movie for me! I opened it up and it said, *Year of the Dog* by Mike White. A movie I never would have gotten offered in mainstream Hollywood, but because Mike knew me personally, he believed I could play the part!

Financiers signed on but their money came with a list of actresses *they* wanted for the lead. Mike told them, "I wrote the movie for Molly and only want to do it with Molly." After that Brad Grey, the head of Paramount, read the script and was interested. Mike told Brad he only wanted me, and Brad said, "Great, I love Molly." And that was that.

I WENT HOME FOR Christmas and my dad flew into a rage while I was helping with the cooking. It was a big scene.

He screamed, "You *ruined* the gravy!"

Whenever he used to yell like that, I'd be really scared. But this time, instead of taking it, I just came right back at him. It was like *This Boy's Life*, when he finally stood up to his stepdad and fired back and decided he was just not gonna take his shit anymore.

I got in his face and said, "Don't you *talk* to me like that. Don't you dare."

I fought back. I finally stood up for myself. And *he* was scared. I made him cry.

I thought, *God, I should have done this a long time ago.*

At home a lot of invoices had piled up for the student loans I had taken out to go to NYU.

As I was opening them up and asking myself how I was ever going to pay, my dad told me I didn't have to worry.

He said, "Oh, they don't keep track of *that*."

So I took my invoices and ripped them up into *tiny* little pieces. Then I threw it in the air saying, "Wheeeeeeee!"

I SAW DEBBIE PALERMO when I was home. She wanted to find a job in casting. So she came to visit me in Los Angeles and decided to stay. I'd been living in Burbank with my friend Lyn Henderson, an actress I first met in NYC and re-met at the SAG bulletin board in LA. Deb moved in with us. Then her brother Mike followed her out and still lives there. He told me recently, "The only reason why I lived in LA was because you lived here already and encouraged me to pursue acting when I graduated high school. Even though Debbie was the first one to suggest I become an actor, it wasn't until Christmas of '88 when you were home for vacation, and you, Deb, and I met for coffee on the east side. You saw my modeling photos and told me I should come to LA."

Debbie ended up getting a job working for Madonna. Lyn worked the night shift at Jerry's Famous Deli. And together, during the day, Lyn and I started "fragrance modeling" all over town.

We'd stand by the escalators at the Sherman Oaks Galleria or some other mall—wherever our booker would send us, all over greater Los Angeles.

For one campaign we dressed up like newsies, with caps and shoulder bags, and shouted, "Extra! Extra! Read all about it! Want to try a spritz of this new fragrance? Notes of pepper and vanilla—you'll get compliments!"

I prayed I wouldn't bump into anyone I knew in my little newsboy outfit.

But I discovered after a month or so that the booking agent never knew whether or not I actually stayed for my shift. She just checked to make sure I showed up at the store. Once I figured this out, I would sign in, wander out into the mall, find a bookstore, and read for a couple hours. Or I would check in and then leave after fifteen minutes. Then I just stopped going at all.

THIS WAS GREAT UNTIL the booker found out. She called and confronted me, asking, "Were you there?" point blank. "Nordstrom just called and said nobody showed up."

"*Yeah, I was there!*"

"Molly, were you or were you *not* at the Santa Ana Nordstrom for your shift?"

I broke down. "*No, Sharon, I wasn't. I'm sorry.*"

"*Molly,* why would you *say* that? Why would you *say* that you were *there* when you weren't *there?*"

"Sharon, *I don't know.* Because I'm a *bad girl.* I'm a *very bad girl.*"

AFTER THAT, Eugene Pack and I both temped at a fancy boutique literary agency on Beverly Drive. They had files on all of their authors—where they liked to eat, what they did in their free time, what they liked to talk about, their spouses' names—so that when the agents took them to dinner, they would have a fun conversation. There were hundreds of interesting realities I learned while temping. There were *hand signals* for "Take a message" and "Be there in two minutes," and "Just get rid of them."

All the while, we were trying to figure out *how* we were going to get in the door as actors. How were we gonna bust in? It was too hard to just slip your picture under an agent's door. A random headshot? No one was ever gonna call. Then we hit on an idea. Eugene had studied with David Mamet. He was (and is) this giant, hugely successful guy, *very* respected—a big-time playwright and screenwriter—but Eugene knew that he wasn't a guy who was in Hollywood much. He just liked staying in Vermont and New York.

We had all these people we wanted to meet in LA: commercial agents, theatrical agents, casting directors. We wanted to be sent out on auditions. So this one Friday we thought of this scam while we were sitting on the floor in the apartment in Burbank I shared with Lyn and Debbie. We decided we would call agents pretending that we worked for David Mamet. First, we did our research. We went to the American Film Institute library and looked up managers and agents that we thought would be good for us in this big, thick agency book. We also looked up actors who we thought were like us, found out who managed them, and decided to go after these people and try to get them to sign us by pretending to be representing Mamet. I called it the Mamet Scam.

For the Mamet Scam, Eugene's fake name was Arnold

Katz and my fake name was Liz Stockwell—and as these characters we called agents, always on Fridays after four, because we knew they'd be in good moods. It's Friday. It's after lunch. Everybody's happy. Getting ready for the weekend. Suddenly, Mamet's thinking about them. They. Are. Delighted.

I'd say, "This is Liz Stockwell calling from David Mamet's office." I was David Mamet's right-hand girl. I was a ray of sunshine. A fun, positive gal.

They would say, "*Oh,* one minute!" and put me directly through to the agent we were pursuing.

Then, when I got the agent on the phone, I would say, "I have this young kid named Eugene Pack that I think you might like."

Flattered that David Mamet was interested in them, they'd all say, "Oh my God, we're so honored that you called us!" And with the upper hand I would go on: "Well, you know, David speaks so highly of your agency and we have a young kid who's part of *our theater* company who David would love for you to meet. David asked me to call YOU specifically, and we'd love for you to meet this kid, who's really special, who you should have an *eye* on."

And they would say, "Of course! Of course! Of course!"

OUR EXPERIENCES IN SELLING health club memberships really helped us with the scam. We knew how to turn a no into a yes. We had it so down that we knew exactly what to say. And we had a rule where you couldn't hang up the phone till you had the appointment in the book.

If there was an obstacle, we had an answer. Just like in sales. In the Mamet Scam there was an answer for *everything.*

Whatever the problem was, we'd find a way to *jump over* it. We had it *all* figured out.

If an agent said, "Well, why don't you have Eugene call me when he gets to town?"

I'd say, "Eugene's really busy: he's rehearsing for David's new play." I would make him the *star* of the new play. "He's running around, having a lot of meetings. Why don't we just set up the appointment now to make it easier on him, so he doesn't have to be worried about that? He's only out here for a few days. He has so many meetings set, I just wanna take care of it *now*."

And they'd be thinking, *Ooh, who is this hot new up-and-coming actor?*

It was just like selling health club memberships: *Don't you fucking hang up until you get that credit card number.*

We were closing. We were finessing the deal as we went along. We had to get the appointment in the books. We couldn't be in the same room while we were on the phone because we would crack each other up. But when I was making my calls, Eugene would listen from outside the door and slide me little notes, and I would do the same thing for him. We started to get so good at the scam.

They would say, "Liz, when you come to town, we should have *lunch*. What's your number?"

And I would say, "*Oh*, I would *looove* to have lunch. We're actually switching offices, but as soon as we're set up in our new place, I'll have my assistant call you."

I never had to give them my number.

This is how I got my start in Hollywood. I'd get Eugene a bunch of appointments and he would get me a bunch of appointments. By Friday at 6:00 we would both have five appointments. Our agreement was that we had to have an equal number set up.

We started meeting everyone—agents at ICM, William Morris. I wanted to be on *Twin Peaks* so Eugene called the casting director, Johanna Ray, and I actually did get cast on *Twin Peaks. Through the Mamet Scam.*

When I met the casting director she just said, "Wonderful! So nice to meet you. I *must* introduce you to David *Lynch!*"

Which was *exactly* what I wanted to have happen. Because I would drive my wreck past her casting office and say, "*Oh, I really want to be on* Twin Peaks. *I love that show!*"

Then she brought me in to audition for Caleb Deschanel, who was the director, and he cast me as Judy Swain, the Happy Helping Hands caseworker.

Eugene also called Bernie Brillstein for me. I wanted to meet Bernie because he was a legend and connected to Lorne Michaels of *Saturday Night Live.*

He said, "How is David? Wonderful. Give him my best!"

Bernie then introduced me to his daughter, Leigh, who was a big agent at ICM.

At that time I thought the Brat Pack was cool. I wanted to be part of the Brat Pack. I wanted to meet Molly Ringwald. So I really had to meet their hot talent manager, who repped all of them. We ran the Mamet Scam on her and set up a meeting. I got all dressed up and was so excited.

When I sat down for my appointment, she glared at me and said, "I just wanted to see what a liar looked like in person."

My heart was pounding. I was in a panic. I had to figure out something quick. I said really naively, "Sorry, I don't know what you're *talking* about."

She said, "Your little friend Arnold *Katz* called me. You know this guy's, like, a total *scammer*."

I just played really innocent: "*What?* I don't know what you're talking about."

She kept glaring and, when I still didn't crack, said, "Can I ask you a question? Are you *dating* this guy?"

I just went with it.

"I am. We've just been dating for, like, a few weeks—you know, like, a month or so. He just said he could help me out and he knows a lot of people in town."

She nodded. "Honey, I've gotta tell you something. This guy is, like, a *scum bucket*. He's a *scam artist*. He doesn't know *anybody, okay*?"

"*Really?*"

"Yeah, *really*. This guy is full of *shit*. Trust me, he can't help you."

I ran out and called Eugene from a pay phone: "We just got *so busted*."

It was the *only* time we got busted, though. Mamet was perfect because everybody knew him but nobody ever saw him. We knew there was never going to be a cross-check.

I haven't ever told this story, because I was always afraid I'd get in trouble, but this is how I started in Hollywood. We ran the Mamet Scam for about six months.

And the way we saw it, we were doing *them* a favor. They were meeting good, young, up-and-coming actors.

Later, if I didn't think my agents were sending me out enough, I would say to Eugene, "We've got to get together on Friday and make phone calls and get more cooking!"

Maybe more women need to push the rules to get to the yes and even out the biased playing field in Hollywood.

CHAPTER 12

Comedy Is King

WORKING IN OFFICES FROM NINE TO FIVE WASN'T SO great for auditioning, and I was getting sick of being indoors and never seeing the sunshine. I started to drive around, looking at restaurants and wondering, *What would it be like to work there?*

So I decided to make the switch. The hours were more flexible.

Cravings was in a great location on Sunset Boulevard in West Hollywood. They had lots of outdoor seating and live piano music. When I filled out an application the owner's wife, Gretchen, was seating customers and she interviewed me right at the hostess stand.

Gretchen also happened to be from Shaker Heights.

She said, "Oh my God, you're from Cleveland!?"

And I was hired.

I ALSO MOVED OUT of the apartment I'd been sharing with Lyn and Debbie Palermo in Burbank and in with a new roommate, a super-Irish-looking, outgoing guy with freckles and pale skin, Brian Donovan. Brian had this appealing, scratchy voice and got a lot of work doing voice-overs for animation and commercials.

At Cravings my hostess stand was right out there on the sidewalk, so I could watch everyone who walked by. I loved being around people. The restaurant was part indoors and part outdoors, so it was always sunny and bright. And I loved listening to the piano when I worked at night.

The boss, Ibrahim, was tough and Turkish and took away my Saturday nights. He was maybe five feet two inches—a short, powerful guy with a sweet side and a self-loathing side. And a notion of how things should be done. He wanted his employees to look a certain way: hair pulled back, nice outfits, clean and put together.

And to get results, he could be tough. He would say exactly what he was thinking—"What is *this*? *You dress like this?*"— and fire employees right on the spot.

If he really needed some leverage, he'd say, "I've been getting complaints about you."

As Ibrahim said those cutting things, he would look right at you. And then he would scoff, "Huh!" Mumbling under his breath, "You have to get *better clothes*."

We were all a little scared of him. But it was such a good job that nobody wanted to leave. I *needed* that job.

I wrote to Alison in Cleveland about it:

> *Debbie is 10,000 in debt. She's thinking of declaring bankruptcy. I'm at least 20,000 in debt with my student loans. Scary. So whenever you start feeling bad about money problems call me or Debbie.*
>
> *Last night my boss at Cravings told me*

A. *that I needed to wear nicer clothes to work*
B. *that he'd gotten complaints about me*

As he was telling me this I kept thinking, "I'm going to quit Right Now." But I swallowed my Pride. It was terrible. . . . I can't afford to quit. I must continue subjecting myself to his moodiness. I am such a prisoner. I felt like such a Loser. Loser.

I'm sorry this letter is so depressing. But facts are stubborn things. Of course I blame my Fate or myself and no one else. And I will pick myself up out of this downward spiral.

WHEN IBRAHIM MADE ME the hostess, I knew it meant he thought of me as capable and strong. I was happy. And I felt honored to have that position—though I also felt guilty because the waiters would have to tip me out.

Of course, he told me, "Since I'm making you the hostess, you need to wear nicer clothes."

There was always that element of fear I wrote to Alison about.

After I bought these clothes, the busboys in the kitchen said, "Oh, Mami, you look *nice* like that. You look *niiice*. Like a *Mexican* mami."

They would also grab me.

I *liked* it. I just thought, *Wonderful. Sweet. They appreciate women and women's bodies. They love women. They like asses and stomachs.*

I *do not* see it that way now. But at the time it made me feel *sexy.* By today's standards, it was misogynistic but back then calling a girl "Mami" and commenting on her figure was the same as giving her flowers.

AS THE HOSTESS, my post was outside, where I looked at the restaurant across the street, Le Petit Four. Ibrahim would always take note of how packed they were. They were his competitors.

One day a woman came in twenty minutes before her lunch reservation.

I recognized her right away. *Wow,* I thought, *it's Jennifer Aniston!*

She was striking: long hair, perfect blowout, crystal-blue eyes, beautiful outfit. I was enamored.

This was right before *Friends,* when she was just on the verge of breaking out. Doing tons of pilots. Lorne Michaels was after her for *SNL.* I was a little hostess from Cleveland and she was this up-and-coming star. I was so impressed. I wanted to know *how* she did it. How was she able to orchestrate her career with such self-assurance at such a young age?

And what I noticed was that she was *all business.* She'd come early because she wanted to make sure she had the right table. In the corner. She set it up for all her agents, and once they arrived, she held court.

Studying her, I thought, *Wow: self-made, hardworking. Getting things done. Just a hot little tamale around town!*

(Telly Savalas was her godfather, too.)

Another time at Cravings, Julia Roberts came in for breakfast with a friend. She looked stunning, just like she did in the movies.

But she just ordered sausage.

Interesting, I thought. *Just sausage. Superstars . . . eat . . . sausage—good to know.*

I thought a lot about it.

Maybe she'd had another breakfast earlier.

Brooke Shields also used to come into Cravings with her

mom, Teri, who'd gotten her daughter cast in the role of a prostitute in *Pretty Baby* when she was twelve. When *I* was a teenager there was a photo book I loved called *The Brooke Book*, which showed Brooke going around to her modeling jobs. And I realized her mother was her talent manager. Her *momager.*

I thought, *I need a momager like Teri Shields to get me out on the town!* My dad didn't know much about that. But he did a little research and said he would try to make a few calls. He got in touch with this agent, Bill Block at ICM. Unfortunately, at the time, Bill Block was a literary agent (now he's a big producer). Still, my dad got me a meeting at ICM just by cold-calling. And then he got me in the door at Young & Rubicam, an ad agency, but it just wasn't the right place.

Teri Shields was also a drinker, which was interesting. At Cravings I would watch her order chardonnay in the afternoon.

One of Brooke's later books was about what a bad alcoholic her mother was.

AT CRAVINGS, I HAD the most fun with my coworkers Jim and Jimmy, cool guys who were in a band together. Both of them were much more than just cool, actually: they were sweet and thoughtful and poetic. And they liked to have fun. We'd come in and eat dinner before our shifts, since it was free, and the creamy chicken Alfredo was so good. We would have parties after work. Cravings was like a family, and we really bonded and had so much fun working together.

I had a big crush on Jimmy, who would arrive on a motorcycle for the dinner shift and change into whites for Ibrahim. He was blond, with serious eyes and a kind face—very sweet and gentle but also funny. Dry, cerebral funny. Jimmy took a real liking to my dad when he came out to LA for a visit and invited the two of us out to dinner.

Jim, who was very tall, with red hair and both his ears and his nose pierced, took his station up front behind a deli counter. He operated the cash register, made salads, and did all the coffees. Jim was on this diet called Fit for Life, eating nothing but fruit all day and then carbs for dinner. It was a popular diet back then.

As I was running back and forth, seating people, I'd pause for a sec to talk with Jim. We'd play the Dirty Question Game.

"Molly, if your boyfriend asked you to lick his asshole, would you?"

I hurried back outside and thought about it as I was seating people. Then I came back to the deli counter.

"If I loved him, and he showered first, *Sure, I'd lick it*," I said.

Emir, one of Ibrahim's Turkish friends, was older than the rest of us, late thirties, and would do anything to make people laugh. And, unlike the rest of us waiters, Emir had impunity with Ibrahim. He could pretty much do whatever he wanted. Emir was *funny*.

"Ibrahim, my brother!" he'd shout while the rest of us were bustling around and worrying about our hair and outfits.

Emir worked double shifts to make extra money, so between lunch and dinner he had to just kill time in the neighborhood.

He spent a lot of time in his car. Then he would come in and say, "I napped. I masturbated!" Emir was like a clown—an Arlecchino.

Cravings was a fucking *joy*.

I loved that place.

It was hard for me to leave that place.

I SIGNED UP FOR improv classes at Second City in Santa Monica, and that's where I met my friend Rob Muir. He was kind of a jock, very all-American—and down-to-earth. We're still close friends. We just clicked, and he quickly became almost like a brother, and an amazing writer-partner. We decided to invite some others from the class and started putting together a comedy group. We started improvising one day a week, coming up with scenes and characters, and started writing a show.

We would meet in my little apartment in Hollywood. And Rob told me something that made a huge impression.

"You know," he said, "comedy is king."

I said, "*Is* it? Is comedy *king*?"

"Yes, it is. The best way to get into show business is through comedy."

"Ooh, but I'm a dramatic actress."

Then I mulled it over and realized I believed him.

Okay, I thought. *Comedy is king.*

WHEN WE DECIDED TO put on a show we called ourselves the Lumber Company. Then Debbie Palermo, who was working in casting on the Warner Bros. lot at the time, told this young agent who she'd really connected with, Steven Levy, that he needed to come see her best friend Molly. She knew I needed representation and she thought he would be the perfect fit. They came to see the show and Steven found me afterward.

"You should be on *SNL*," he said.

He begged me, "Please, come have a meeting with me."

I did. The agency where he worked was named Herb Tannen & Associates. When I got there I noticed that everything was *little*. In the waiting room they had these tiny red chairs. And the tables were so low, my knees towered above them.

Sitting on these little tables were copies of *Highlights* magazine.

Herb Tannen & Associates was a children's agency.

Steven came into the waiting room and said, "Let's go out on the patio."

We did, and as he smoked cigarette after cigarette, he told me, "Yes, this *is* a children's agency, but I've been asked by Herb to start an adult division. I think you should be on *SNL*, and I'm gonna get you there."

I saw that he was really passionate and that he believed in me. When I met Steven, I thought he could do business in a phone booth. He didn't even need a fancy office. So I signed on as his client. And it turned out that he did have one other adult client, Brad Garrett, who was a stand-up comedian and went on to be a regular on *Everybody Loves Raymond*.

Then the Lumber Company got a review in *Backstage* and I was singled out. That was *very* exciting. So Rob and I decided to do our own show, just the two of us. We called it the Rob and Molly Show. At first we took turns performing. He would do a character; I would do a character. But over time it was Rob who wanted the show to focus more on me, something that I never would have pushed for myself. But he helped me take that space.

AS ROB WROTE ME RECENTLY,

In our comedy group you stood out because you weren't doing jokes, you were doing characters, not caricatures. Sure, some of your characters were over-the-top, but they were always rooted in truth. You not only found the humor in the characters, but humanity. You weren't afraid to take a break from the comedy and explore the bittersweet sadness in the character. Then once you pulled the audience in, you turned on a dime and surprised them with something quirky and offbeat. No one else was doing that kind of comedy. It was brave and unapologetic. You weren't about zingers and catch phrases, you dug deep and created three dimensional characters. I always thought you were a cross between Carol Burnett and Gilda Radner.

You were fearless and willing to take chances, always pushing the boundaries. I wanted to team up with you for three reasons; your infectious energy, your passion and work ethic, and lastly you loved to play on stage. Performers have different reasons for being on stage, but to me it seemed like you were there to play and have fun. And that's what we did.

I thought the show should focus on you because you were something unique. Not a lot of women at the time were really willing to let their guard down. You could be dark and edgy, lewd and crude, totally outrageous. You didn't care about how you appeared on stage, because it wasn't you. You weren't playing a part; you became the character. Your performances were riotously funny. I remember when you were doing Mary Katherine one night and you cut your hand on stage, you never stopped, didn't even pause, you were so deep in the character that you just went on.

There was an electricity when you hit the stage. Nothing was predictable, the audience (even me sometimes) never knew what was going to happen next. I knew you were headed for great things and I wasn't going to get in the way.

I remember before our shows became popular, you were thinking of going back to doing theater, and I said no! Comedy is King. In the early 90's there weren't any

*females doing the kind of character comedy you were
doing. I knew if you could be seen by the right people,
you'd be on your way.*

THE SHOW WAS A tight fifty minutes. You're in and out. I figured people were busy. Agents were busy. I thought about
their long days working at the office. They were on the phone
all the time, so I was constantly thinking about how to cater
to them, to get them to my show. Thinking about their lives.
My goal was for just one industry person to come per show.
A realistic goal. We made the show very friendly for busi-
nesspeople. I would think about them coming home from
work and wanting to relax and have fun, so we'd always serve
alcohol. We had a saxophone player and a keyboard player
accompanying us. I paid for the music with my hostessing
money. We made it like a party, at a convenient time so people would drive straight from their offices in Beverly Hills. I
would *just* think about making it fun. You get to come, watch
a show, have a glass of wine, go meet a friend for dinner after
the show. Easy-peasy. Don't bore them with some loooooong
show. And that formula *did* work, I have to say.

I would pack the house myself. I would tell every single
customer I met at Cravings, "Oh, you've got to come see my
show!"

I'd ask, "What's your name? Oh, Jamie. Okay. And what's
your boyfriend's name? Ben? Oh, oh my God, he's a lawyer?"
And I would take notes. And since this was before email, I
kept a *big* box of names and phone numbers, so when I did a
show, I got on the phone and started dialing and dialing and
did not stop. I would call and say, "Hi, Jamie? Yeah, I met you
at Cravings. I want you and your boyfriend, Ben, to come see

my show." I would make five hundred calls to get two hundred people to come, and hustle and tell *everyone* I met: "You gotta come see my show!" And I would pack the house so it would look like a good, hot show for the industry people who came. There was nothing more important than packing the house. Pack it, pack it, pack it, pack it!

One night I met this vivacious and funny woman named Lisa Sundstedt at a party. So I invited her and not only did she come but she *flipped* for it and from then on would spread the word and invite so many people. It was Lisa who introduced me to these three guys who sang R&B a cappella together under the name TMT. I ended up putting them in the show and the audience loved it. And Lisa and I became good friends.

I also invited homeless people. *Everybody should be allowed to come,* I thought.

Steven Levy remembers that there were homeless people with no teeth who would come and say to him when he was working the door, "Molly invited us to the show. We're here for Molly."

I was always nice to people who collected cans and asked for food and they would take the bus to see my show.

Debbie Palermo came to every single one of my shows. She was always so encouraging and supportive. I included little inside jokes for her. And her brother Mike could always calm me down before I performed, telling me not to worry. He'd take me to Denny's and we'd talk it out. He was a constant support.

Once, before one of my stage shows, Deb saw me on the street and said, "There she is . . . Superstar!" It became a refrain. And from then on I would always say "Superstar!" to her—because I knew she *loved* it. She coined it.

AND IF PEOPLE COULDN'T afford to buy a ticket I would pay for their ticket. I was really into creative visualization. I thought, *Someday the money's gonna come back to me.* I believed if I put it out, it would come back to me tenfold. And on the flip side, deep down I was petrified. I had a fear that everything was going to blow up the way it had when I was little. I was afraid that anything good was not going to last: *Oh my God, I'm not going to be able to do my show because what if my tooth starts throbbing and then I'm going to need instant dental surgery and I'll have to cancel the show.* I remember driving to the west side on the 10 Freeway with my wigs in the back seat, and I was *nervous.* Doing these shows was a lot of pressure. So, to be on the safe side, I would invite my dentist, Dr. Karen Nakagawa, to some of my shows just in case I needed an emergency root canal. It calmed me down knowing she was in the audience. She didn't always come, but when she did, she was like a talisman (and an excellent dentist).

WE MADE MARY KATHERINE Gallagher an actress auditioning for a new David Lynch movie. I'd do a free-form improv as this character trying to get cast in the movie, and Rob's character would try to get me offstage after I got too crazy. My audition outfit was a blue-and-white-striped T-shirt, cat glasses just like Ann Ranft's, red Keds, and a red headband. I combined how I felt when I was little with what Ann physically looked like, with her lazy eye and her eye patch. And in my mind Mary Katherine Gallagher is an adult child of an alcoholic who always feels like she's in trouble.

I would do wild stuff, physical stuff. It was like punk rock. I wanted to hurt myself. I was in a reckless stage of my life. Sometimes I would climb the walls, or cut my leg and bleed, and I would always bruise myself. I liked being roughed up. I would get so into the performance that I couldn't feel any pain. I made my entrance by tripping over a folding chair, which I'd pick up and drag toward center stage to announce, "Hi, I'm Mary Katherine Gallagher."

There were certain physical beats that I always followed and improvised around. After the chair I'd be very bashful. So Rob would prod me by saying, "Go ahead, Mary. Step out in front and tell us who you are."

Then I'd tell Rob, "My grandmother says that I bear a very, very striking resemblance to a young Elizabeth Taylor," which my dad actually told me. So my dad *was* the grandmother. And I'd do a dramatic monologue.

Then I'd say, "You know, I can do gymnastics," and I would jump in the air and do a split.

But then I'd get too carried away and he'd have to scold me, "Mary—Mary Katherine Gallagher—get down right now from that scaffold right this minute." And it would fucking *kill*. The audience would go nuts. They loved that I didn't care about bruising myself or making myself bleed. I just committed with my full heart.

I don't like it when performers act like they are making fun of their characters. I believe that even with comedy you should still play the emotional truth of what your character wants, and who they are, because it anchors the comedy and gives it an emotional depth that makes the comedy stronger, richer. I treat the comedy the same way I would treat a serious dramatic performance.

I GOT A VERY positive response from my show. People would come up after and say, "I *loved* your show!"

But I always felt like there was an ache in my heart. Like someone was missing. My mom. There was this longing. A terrible ache. I couldn't quite be happy. I couldn't take it in that people liked it. I was driven to keep doing the shows and to work harder.

THANKS TO STEVEN, *Saturday Night Live* asked for a five-minute tape of my characters. He had gotten out the word.

I said, "Why do they need a tape? Can't they come see the show?"

"No, they want a tape."

I used all my waitressing money and I made a tape. I worked very hard on it, paying a guy to direct and edit it, and didn't have much money after. And I knew a couple of other comedy women whose tapes were being sent in.

I remember being on a pay phone near my apartment, on Fountain and Vine, across from the El Pollo Loco, when Steven said the words, "Lorne Michaels is going to pass."

I was devastated.

I just cried and cried.

But now I'm sure Lorne never even saw that tape.

When Steven told me who they *had* picked to audition for Lorne, I just thought, *Oh, whatever.*

I guess her tape was better.

Then I thought, *You know what? I'm just gonna work really hard on my show, develop an arsenal of characters, so that when* SNL *comes back around again, I'm gonna be locked and loaded and ready.*

And it does show that everything happens for a reason. Because I feel like if I'd gotten *SNL* at that time, it wouldn't have been right, because it wasn't the best time for women.

CHAPTER 13

SNL

AFTER I'D GOTTEN PASSED OVER, I CONTINUED DEVELOPING and writing my stage show. I worked on an old character named Ruby Daly, who had a brace on her leg and was obsessed with Natalie Wood. And Sally O'Malley, who was a combination of my dad, and a woman from my neighborhood growing up and a little Miss Patty and Miss Jackie (the choreographer sisters). She sang "Hello, Dolly!" as a tribute to the memory of her dead husband, Jack O'Malley. The love Sally O'Malley expressed for Jack was actually me thinking about how much I loved and adored my dad. I would buy a fresh black pre-teased wig from the same wig woman on Vine Street in Hollywood before each show. I also bought red polyester pants at a thrift shop, and a yellow shirt. I would pull the red pants up really high and stick my stomach out. This got a big laugh. And I thought people were laughing at my stuck-out stomach. But then I realized they were actually laughing at the ancillary camel toe created by the pants-hiking. It was an accident. And I felt a little embarrassed. But I decided to keep it in because it really got laughs.

I also kept working on Mary Katherine, honing the character. Taking notes. Paying attention to what got a laugh. What didn't work. I wrote from within. The character is basically an exaggerated version of myself as a kid—as a teen girl. I was always really focused on what I was learning as a comedian. I learned the character in front of the audience. I wanted to develop, develop, develop. After each show the next day, I'd walk around the block and review the whole performance in my head, revising according to how the audience had responded to every joke, and I would keep adjusting it—going through each beat. A process I think of as oral writing. Then I'd actually write out notes and follow them for the next live show.

One time while performing Mary Katherine Gallagher I said, "Sometimes when I get nervous, I stick my fingers under my arms and smell them, like that—but that's *bad*!"

Which was based on something that really happened. Ann Ranft and I were in West Palm Beach, on vacation, by the pool at a Holiday Inn. I noticed that my armpits smelled and we had this real teen puberty moment together where we said to each other, "Can I smell yours? I want to. And you can smell mine."

And I thought, *Note to self: that got a laugh.* So it became a part of my performance, which always followed the same structure: shy, warms up, goes crazy, gets sent away. But in the end she would get the part.

It was like a little dance of hope. Mary Katherine's trying really hard, then she gets too carried away. She misbehaves and sabotages herself. The auditioner sends her away. But then he decides, "You got the part." And she succeeds. The original sketch was a little dance of survival.

I WAS ALWAYS TAKING notes about how Mary Katherine Gallagher should act, little rules for myself.

From one of those notebooks:

- She enters from the doorway tripping over a chair.

- She falls.

- She drags the chair.

- She feels embarrassed.

- With her head down she puts the chair back in its proper place.

- She introduces herself: Mary Katherine Gallagher x3.

- Pick a moment to look at audience, scared, cry, shake. Really look at the audience when you are shy.

- She hides behind the auditioner.

- He forces her to come to the front. He says sweet things to encourage her.

- She keeps her head down and shakes.

- Shy, shy, shy, shy, almost starting to cry.

- She puts her hands and fingers under her underarms and then smells her fingers sticking them in her nostrils.

- She squeezes her boobs nervously. She says, "When I get nervous I touch my boobs."

- She picks and pulls at her underwear.

- Slowly gets warmed up.

- Story about grandmother, kids making fun of me,

saying, "Here comes Mary Katherine Gallagher and her dumb, crippled grandmother."

- She says, "My grandmother tells me I bear a very striking resemblance to a young Elizabeth Taylor."

- Does gymnastics.

- Auditioner asks if she has a song.

- She sings "Sometimes When We Touch."

- Gets too carried away.

- She gets stuck on a wall: "I'm stuck! I'm stuck!"

- He gets her down.

- He says, "You are very bad! I'm writing your name down."

- Somewhere around here she exits, realizing she has gotten out of control.

- After she's gone the auditioner says, "Let's take a break."

- Important: stakes should be high. What she wants is like life or death. The audience must know what she wants. What her heart desires.

While I worked on my stage show, I was also auditioning for TV, usually "best friend" parts on series. I got rejected a lot. A lot. Like, a lot. The casting directors for those shows didn't seem to know what to do with me. With so much rejection, I was getting disillusioned about the town and how hard it all was. But deep down I knew I was right for something more than just playing some supportive best friend part on TV. ("Don't worry, he's gonna call you back—I just *know* it.") There were three hundred actresses with pretty curls—who had mommies—who could do that. What I really wanted to do was the type of comedy I was developing in my stage show.

When I auditioned for Tropicana Pure Premium orange juice, I did a version of Sally O'Malley from my stage show. And that landed me a national commercial. The role was a diner waitress serving customers orange juice.

After I poured, they said, "This sure tastes like fresh-squeezed orange juice!"

And I replied, deadpan, "Nope, it's Tropicana Pure Premium."

I wrote a letter to a friend saying, "My Tropicana commercial is running. It makes me look fat. They shot it from under my chin and when I first saw it I secretly hoped it wouldn't run but now I'm happy and I like doing characters. I don't wanna be one of those actresses who has to be worried about getting old and looking good."

I DECIDED I DIDN'T want to focus too much on auditioning, because they weren't really getting what I did. I wanted to focus on writing and creating *original* characters. And because it was so hard for me to get cast in the best-friend roles, I felt so much urgency when it came to creating original material to put in my show. I figured if you are a woman who knows how to write, that's better, because then you aren't just waiting to fit into something that somebody else wrote that might not even be right for you. Better to just do your own material.

Comedy could also be a boys' club. That was a frequent criticism. But I just thought, *Why are these comedy girls putting up with these little parts? Just go create your own. Otherwise you're going to play these little, nothing roles in these boys' comedy shows. I'm not going to do that. That's not going to get me anywhere.*

The struggle forced me to create my own work. It felt very empowering to stop relying so much on auditions.

If I *had* gotten one of those jobs as the best friend on some multi-cam sitcom, I never would have pushed myself to create my own work and develop my stage show. So it ended up being positive, this struggle, never having an easy time.

I got little parts here and there. And I did eventually get a development deal out of my stage show, from Carolyn Strauss at HBO. I was thrilled. Carolyn was my first big supporter! But then that ended up falling apart. And I just remember thinking, *This is so fucking hard.* I was starting to question everything. *I don't know if I have the heart for this,* I thought.

A casting director, Kathleen Letterie, called me in for an audition. She had helped me get a part on *The John Larroquette Show* a few years earlier. When I went in this time she said, "Molly, you really need a break. You've been around town for *a while.*"

It was rough to hear, but I thought, *She's right.*

I FINALLY QUIT CRAVINGS, after four years, because I realized I was getting too associated with the place. I got so well-known around LA as the hostess there that people would shout, "Grilled lemon chicken salad!" when they saw me.

I thought, *I've been here four and a half years and I'm ready to leave. I'm going to do it. I'm going to take a chance. I'm gonna give my notice.*

I didn't really have anything specific lined up. I was getting some parts. But still, it wasn't like a guarantee. I knew it was the right time to just take a chance and leave. It was a big thing to leave a place that had been stable for me for so many years.

When I went up to Ibrahim's office and told him that I was leaving, he gave me this look. He knew that we had had tough times.

"*Molly,*" he said. Then he knelt down and *kissed my hands.*

"Thank you, Ibrahim," I said.

After that, I drove to Pan Pacific Park and listened to "In Your Eyes" by Peter Gabriel over and over again on my Sony Walkman. It was really windy. I kept rewinding the song. I could feel that change was in the air. There was a kind of magic in the night. One of *those* nights. It was a very profound moment. I knew it was time. *I'm gonna take a chance and get out of here.*

I really embraced the unknown. That was the spirit. Not knowing what lay ahead.

I could feel that my life was going to change.

My sister Mary sent me a letter around the time I was struggling. She said, "Hang in there. I feel you are destined for success. I'm not B.S.ing—really."

AFTER I LEFT, I worked at the Melrose Baking Company, which was across the street from the Groundlings, a famous improv school, where *SNL* found a lot of their cast members. This woman I met in an improv class, named Pat Cotter, took classes at the Groundlings, and she was a really good writer. One day she said, "There's this kid who's in Groundlings who you would really click with. Do you mind if I bring him over to Melrose Baking Company?"

That was Will Ferrell. I waited on him.

I said, "Nice to meet you, Will."

And I gave him scones.

I KEPT ON AUDITIONING for parts. Auditioning was a piece of the pie—not the main goal, but a part of my overall plan. I wasn't waiting around for auditions but of course if I got one I would go. One time I got called in to meet the producers of a show called *Hunter* for a very small part. Just one line.

I had to say, "This is Sergeant Hunter and Sergeant Mc-Call; they are police officers."

Eugene warned me that one-line auditions were the worst. And he was right! I had to *sell* that one little line to four producers and one casting director—and I still didn't get the job.

Another time I drove Eugene to a callback for Chevrolet. He'd already had an audition and they wanted to see him again. They'd instructed him to dress up like an Orthodox Jewish rabbi: side curls, yarmulke, robes.

At the audition I was checking out all the other rabbis and whispering to Gene, "It's *yours*."

When the audition was over I was so convinced he was going to get it we went out and celebrated over iced teas at a '50s-style diner. And *he got it*. He was so excited. Chevrolet had to file what's called a Taft-Hartley report, since Eugene wasn't in SAG-AFTRA, meaning the producers had to explain their reason for hiring him instead of a union member and send the union his headshot and résumé. We were clueless but learning so much about how it all worked.

I still didn't have a commercial agent. But I had meetings with William Morris and Abrams-Rubaloff & Lawrence—two biggies.

Rejection.

Rejection.

I was heartbroken for about fifteen minutes. My dad was actually more upset than I was.

I told him, "They didn't sign me because I'm not blond and beautiful." And he gave me a talking-to.

"Well, Molly, if that's what you want to think, you'll *never* get a commercial agent. That's the easy way out."

He was a tough cookie.

I fought him for a while until I realized he was right.

I was so excited when I got to audition for *Seinfeld*—a big deal. I knew that if they liked you they'd cast you in the part that same day. They called in very talented women for that show, and because it was so popular, they got the best comedy performers in town to come in and read. All the other actresses in the waiting room could tell who was staying and who was *not* asked to stay after an audition, because if they were interested, you'd be asked to stick around and then at 5:30 head over to another building on the lot to read for the producers. Otherwise you'd read once and nobody would ask you to stay for a second reading.

I didn't get asked to stay. Then I ran into Katherine La-Nasa, another actress I knew, in the parking lot. She had been auditioning for something else. Now she was doing ballet stretches by her car. Not a care in the world.

I wished I could be breezy and casual with auditions like her, and not let all the endless rejection get to me.

But. I. Couldn't.

She said, "Molly, how are you doing? What's going on?"

How *was* I doing?

I was sliding down into a dark depression.

I had just heard the casting director for *Seinfeld* say, "Thanks for coming in, Molly!"

Then I had tried to act cheery in front of all the other actresses waiting to still go in to read as I walked out to this parking lot. I'd said, "Bye, everyone!!! Good luck!!!"

My sinking heart.

My disappointment.

Oh.

Well.

Ugh.

I watched Katherine do her ballet pliés.

And thought to myself, *I'm gonna buy a half a chicken at Gelson's and go home and close my shades. I really don't know if I can do this anymore. I don't think I have the heart for this. There is too much rejection. It hurts my heart too much.*

I'd been trying and trying for so long.

I decided to take a year off. I stopped doing my show. I didn't hustle. I just pulled back and kind of let go. I was getting rejected a lot. Grasping so hard wasn't working. I was close to giving up. Maybe I didn't have what it took.

That's when the call came, of course.

MARCI KLEIN, THE DAUGHTER of Calvin Klein, was the head of the talent department and also a producer for *SNL*. She was fierce, sexy, no-bullshit, with long blond hair—and so smart.

They were looking for new cast members. Marci had gotten close to my manager, Steven Levy. She thought he was so funny and loved talking on the phone with him. She called and asked for an audition tape. I wasn't going to submit another tape. It was too easy a way for them to say no to me again. I said she needed to come *see* my stage show if she was interested. If they wanted to consider me, they were gonna have to come see me perform live. This time I was gonna do it my way. I was a more mature performer. I was more ready.

She agreed. I called my partner Rob. He was a full-time writer at this point and didn't really want to put up our show again. We hadn't done the show for a year.

I begged him.

"Please, Rob, just do this one, please! I'll pay for the band. I'll do everything. Just show up."

"Sure," he said. Always reliable and wonderful.

FIVE YEARS EARLIER there had been a woman with her own casting business who would recommend comedians to Lorne Michaels, because she knew him. She kind of declared herself a scout for *SNL*, though it wasn't official. Unfortunately, this woman didn't seem to be very interested in women—which made sense, because it was a time when women weren't represented on the show strongly. I remember thinking, *She's missing all the good women.*

But now, lucky for me, that woman wasn't as involved. Marci Klein was looking for new talent herself and got in touch directly. I was thrilled.

Finally, I thought. *Maybe I'll have a shot.*

I could always psychologically analyze a hurdle I needed to get over and figure out the problem. When the other woman was going around LA, looking for talent for all those years, I'd thought, *I gotta jump over this lady. I don't think she's gonna help me.*

Now we basically set up the whole show just for Marci. I had twenty-four hours' notice. And that show was fucking solid. We rocked the house. Paid three hundred bucks for the band.

Marci later told an interviewer that Steven Levy "called me *constantly*. He kind of harassed me, but he was very funny about it. And he *begged me*, *begged me*, to see her in Santa Monica. Picked me up at my hotel and drove me there. And that's how I found Molly Shannon. Her live show was one of the greatest *ever*."

MARCI FOUND ME AFTER the show and said, "Come out for dinner with me."

She took me out to the Ivy. I was over the moon. The restaurant was fancy and fun and on the beach. Marci was wonderful and funny and so down-to-earth—no-nonsense. I brought along Mike Palermo, Debbie's brother. When I'd been feeling like quitting, Mike had told me, "Molly, it's impossible for you to stop, because by nature you are a performer. Being a performer is not the same thing as being an actor. Your calling is more specific and your true nature would never allow you to do anything but perform." Mike has always had the ability to cut right to the truth of anything in a crystal-clear way.

At dinner Marci said, "You're coming to New York to audition for *SNL*."

I couldn't believe it. *Yippeeeee!!!*

Then the woman who wasn't so interested in women got wind that Marci was flying me to New York City to audition. And she had advice for me. She warned me, "Whatever you do, don't do that character Mary Katherine Gallagher when you go to audition. If you do, you will never ever get hired. Lorne will hate that. He will hate that dirty little character. Don't do it. You'll never get the job."

I thought, *Out of my way!*

But, to be safe, I said "Okay."

MARCI WAS SO NICE. She said, "If you have any questions—if you want any tips—call me."

And in the weeks leading up to my audition, I took advantage and called Marci at NBC every few days. She was unbelievably gracious and helpful.

I asked her, "Would it be okay if I flew my partner, Rob Muir, in to perform with me?"

She said, "Yeah, bring your partner."

I asked, "Can we wear wigs?"

"Yeah, wear a wig."

"What should I do? What kind of characters? I don't really do impressions."

"Do whatever you want."

She liked that I was asking her for help and she really guided me.

SNL wanted to find somebody.

THEY FLEW ME TO New York first-class and put me up at the Paramount Hotel. It was *soooooo* exciting. It was also nerve-wracking, because there were all these other performers flying out to New York City to audition, too. We were all on the same flight. But I just remember thinking, *I can't believe that I've come this far. I'm a girl from Cleveland, Ohio, who really struggled and went through hard times. Just the fact that I'm being flown to New York City, being put up at the Paramount Hotel, to audition for* Saturday Night Live *is incredible!* It felt like a spiritual experience. I just felt so grateful to have gotten this far. *What an honor,* I thought. It was "a real feather in my cap," as my dad said.

They put our group, almost entirely women, onstage at a comedy club called Stand Up NY in front of Lorne, Marci, producer Jim Downey, and Chris Farley. We each got five or six minutes and it was a very tough crowd—all tourists who thought they were going to see stand-up comedy and instead found themselves wondering, *What is this? Sketch comedy?*

Before going on, they had us all penned up in a little narrow hallway to the side of the stage and it was hysteria. The other performers were saying to me, "You brought wigs? *I* didn't bring wigs. You brought your comedy partner? I didn't know we could do that."

I tried not to let anyone get to me. I just said I'd called Marci Klein and she'd told me I could do all this stuff. A good friend I'd met at drama school at NYU, Andrew Shaifer, came with me to the audition and kept me grounded.

When people were lining up and starting to get competitive, he said "Kid, let's just get out of here until it's your turn." Andrew and Rob Muir and I walked around the block over and over again.

Rob told me, "After tonight, your life is going to change."

Andrew kept checking in to make sure I wouldn't miss my slot. I was nervous. He kept me calm. I'm so thankful to Andrew and Rob.

I decided to just enjoy the process. That nothing was going to upset me.

I got my turn near the end of the night. I don't know if I was last or second to last. I had decided to try to do five characters in the five or so minutes allotted. I walked out and immediately saw Chris Farley.

This is the coolest, I thought. I was so jazzed.

But then, as I started my first character, nobody was laughing. Crickets. I thought to myself, *Oh my God, I'm tanking.* It was a tough crowd.

So I gave myself a quick pep talk: *Just be a good actress. Do your best job. Just commit as an actress. Don't worry if you don't get laughs. Just commit with your heart and do it.* I told myself this during the five seconds while I was turning around with my back to the audience and putting on a new character's glasses. I kneeled down to put the glasses on . . . slooowly, calmly, deep breath, *It's okay, Molly.* . . . Then I turned back around—*Shoop!*—and it went *great.*

Since I had temped for a famous agent, the one who always sent Eugene out for cheesecake, I decided to do an impression of her, using her real name. I probably should not have done that. It was an inside thing. I was so green, I didn't really know better. But halfway through I looked at Lorne and Marci and they were dying laughing. I don't think they could believe it. They knew this agent well and seemed to like my impression.

For my five minutes I did the character I had created in my stage show, Sally O'Malley, but as Ann Miller, the famous tap dancer, to show them I could do celebrity impressions. I also did Lisa Marie Presley. And since Rob Muir and I had played these perky talk show hosts in the Rob and Molly Show for years—my character was called Sunny Daze—I also did her. But I did *not* do Mary Katherine Gallagher for my audition. Just in case that talent scout was right.

Hmmmmmm.

After my audition, I felt very peaceful and happy. I felt very good knowing that I did the best job I could do.

I went back to LA, and so many people I knew were saying, "I heard you're gonna get hired for *Saturday Night Live*."

I said, "Not as far as I know."

But I wondered, *Could this be true?*

Months passed. I didn't hear anything.

Lorne usually has you come back for a meeting when he is pretty sure he's going to hire you. I got a call asking if I could fly back to New York City to meet Lorne. They picked me up in a big black stretch limousine at my apartment in Hollywood. *Oh. My. God. Thrilling.*

On the plane to New York, first-class again, I sat next to this young, very intelligent, serious businessman.

"I'm going to meet Lorne Michaels," I told him. "How should I approach that meeting? Do you have any tips?"

"Ask him opinion questions," he told me. "Don't ask questions that would just get a one-word answer. Don't talk all about yourself. Ask him what he thinks about stuff." And now that I know Lorne, I realize that was the greatest advice ever. He loves giving his opinions about stuff.

The businessman offered me his card when we got off the plane and I took it and put it in my wallet.

And I did what he suggested.

People get nervous being in front of Lorne, and they try really hard to be funny, and it ends up being such a turnoff. I was more serious in my meeting and asked his opinion about a lot of stuff. Because of that, we had a great meeting. It was thrilling meeting him. I'd had a dream years before that I met him in a line, standing and waiting outside, against a wall. We started talking and got along well. It was a fantastic dream.

Near the end of my meeting Lorne said, "I should warn you that a lot of the cast members get upset if they're not in sketches."

"I promise if I ever get hired I won't complain if I'm not in anything," I told him. "I will just be so grateful." And I meant it.

He said, "Well, you'll see."

And I left feeling like he was watching out for me.

I WAS SO HAPPY about how well the interview had gone that I went over to my sister's apartment in TriBeCa to celebrate. Mary had gotten married and had given birth to a beautiful baby girl, Shannon Katherine, while I'd been in LA. Mary, her husband, Brian, and I all had a glass of pinot noir together to toast my good meeting, and then I left to go back to my hotel.

And when I got out onto Duane Street, I got mugged—thrown down on the ground by a jacked-up, wired, very tall drug addict who just whipped me off my feet. But I was so excited that I'd just met Lorne that I didn't even care!

He seemed nervous, eyes darting around to make sure nobody could see him mugging me. "Give me your wallet. Give me your wallet," he whispered in my ear. I could feel his tongue.

I thought, *Oh my God. So this is what it's like to be mugged. This is interesting. He seems nervous, too! I will be like water!*

"Take whatever you want!" I said. "Do you want my coat?"

He said, "Nah. That's okay. You can keep your coat."

It was a little Stockholm syndrome moment—pure terror mixed with *Oh-he's-being-thoughtful-while-he-mugs-me* bonding—like *Awww, he's sweet! He's letting me keep my coat! What a sweetie pie. He's a gentleman after all.*

And the next morning I got a call from the businessman I'd met on the plane. He was worried because a homeless guy had found his business card and called him saying he'd found my wallet on the ground. I told him what had happened and that I was okay.

I flew back to Los Angeles still not knowing anything.

Then Steven Levy, who'd worked so hard to get me the audition, showed up and banged on my apartment screen door one night, smelling like In-N-Out burgers and cigarettes. He walked into my studio and said, "You got *Saturday Night Live!*"

PART THREE

BABY, THIS IS IT

CHAPTER 14

Showing Them

I WENT FROM WORKING IN A RESTAURANT TO DOING *SATURDAY Night Live*. From making five hundred calls to get two hundred people to come to my live show—hustling and telling everybody, "Come see my show! Come see my show!"—to being seen by millions of people.

Before I moved to New York, I took that big box of names and phone numbers I'd used to pack the house for my stage show and I threw it in a dumpster. I thought, *I don't have to call everyone and invite them—they can just tune in!*

SNL SENT ANOTHER BIG black stretch limo to pick me up at my duplex apartment in Hollywood. It was like a movie. My roommate and friend, Brian Donovan, was taking pictures as I got in and was whisked away.

In New York City they put me up at the Paramount Hotel again. It was like one of those montages: Marci Klein, the fun, cool, new friend who made me over, cut my hair, got my makeup done, found me new clothes that were stylish and chic.

"Get rid of the red tights! Get rid of these little-girl dresses!

You're gonna go to Frédéric Fekkai and Oscar Blandi is gonna cut your hair," she said.

Then I moved and found my own sunny apartment downtown. The guy who showed it to me said it was a "lucky apartment." After that, I bought a new piece of furniture, something I'd never done before—a sofa bed.

DURING MY FIRST LIVE SHOW, in Studio 8H at Rockefeller Center, as everybody was bustling around, I called Mary from the house phone. I was at the NBC page desk talking with her when Chris Farley walked by.

"Chris," I asked, "can you say hi to my sister?"

He grabbed the phone and said, "Hello, Mary!"

It was bananas. It was so exciting.

"Mary, can you *believe* that was *Chris Farley*?"

Chris always kneeled down and prayed before every show. He was a Catholic like us. Erin Maroney, one of the writers, used to say that Lorne loved Irish Catholics. Conan O'Brien, Colin Jost, Chris Farley, Jimmy Fallon, Julia Sweeney, Colin Quinn, Kevin Nealon, Tim Herlihy, John Mulaney . . . The list goes on and on.

I prayed—and took a single bite of a pretzel with mustard—before *every single show*, too.

IT ALL *REALLY* HIT ME after *SNL*'s longtime announcer, Don Pardo, enunciated my name in the opening credits: "*M o l l y S h a n n o n!*" It was thrilling. It never got old. I would stand by the TV monitor and listen to him every Saturday, watching the opening montage, just savoring it. I felt so grateful. Every. Single. Time.

Don had been the *SNL* announcer from the very beginning. Lorne is loyal to people who really pull their own weight on the show, cares about their families, and looks out for them. *That's* Lorne.

Don always had on the lucky red socks he'd worn for every broadcast since getting sober. We'd talk a little before he went into the booth to announce the cast while the montage played.

George Clooney was the host of my first show. I was in the opening monologue, playing the part of his assistant, and I remember thinking, *Oh my God, this is so cool.* Saturday Night Live *has an amazing band, and I don't have to pay for it myself with my waitressing money.*

I had Gilda Radner's old dressing room.

Lorne sent me flowers and a note that said, "Welcome to *Saturday Night Live.* I'm really glad you're here."

It made my head explode.

A REPORTER FOR *NEW YORK* MAGAZINE was doing a piece on *SNL* right when I started. He'd pitched it saying, "I'm gonna do a *great* article on the show." And Lorne had given him full access—which he does not give to reporters. This guy interviewed everyone. Then he trashed the show, claiming it was falling apart.

I'd started in February. It was *SNL*'s twentieth season, and the repertory players were Ellen Cleghorne, Chris Elliott, Chris Farley, Janeane Garofalo, Norm Macdonald, Michael McKean, Mark McKinney, Tim Meadows, Mike Myers, Kevin Nealon, Adam Sandler, and David Spade, plus featured players Al Franken, Laura Kightlinger, Jay Mohr, and me. The piece came out in March. There was a photo on the magazine's cover of Chris Farley wearing a TV set on his head. The tagline was "The Inside Story of the Decline and Fall of *Saturday Night Live*." And it was big news.

Lorne was furious. He felt like the writer did a bait and switch.

At the end of the season he was forced to undertake one of the biggest cast overhauls in the show's history. Certain contracts were not renewed.

THE LAST SHOW OF THAT SEASON, one of the Irish Catholic writers, Tim Herlihy, helped me do a "Weekend Update" where I played Norm Macdonald's sixth-grade grammar teacher. My dad thought Norm was fantastic and said to me, "Boy, oh boy, he is movie star handsome."

That was a phrase my dad loved: "movie star handsome." For the "Weekend Update" I was doing an imitation of a woman who lived next to my grandmother. She would get really drunk in the afternoon. Then she'd call handymen on the phone to settle scores.

The drunker she got, the more *grammatical* she would get.

"Listen up!" she would say. "Your, quote, 'lawn boy,' unquote, never showed up to mow my lawn today and I'm furious! Exclamation point! I received *i* before *e* except after *c* an invoice and he never showed up. Period."

Maybe because my "Update" appearance went well, they kept me on for their twenty-first season.

I got upgraded from feature player to full-time cast member and was brought back with returning cast members Mark McKinney, David Spade, Tim Meadows, Norm Macdonald, and a new regime.

Lorne presented a group of brand-new talent, and I made the cut.

In a review on the *Onion*'s *A.V. Club* website, Erik Adams and Alex McLevy wrote, the show's "transition from the Bad Boys era to this big-and-broad time of outsized characters is very much in keeping with the cultural transitions of the time . . ."

Colin Quinn was writing and performing, and Fred Wolf and Steve Higgins were the head writers.

Then, soon after that, Tracy Morgan and Ana Gasteyer joined.

The feeling was: *Fresh blood.*

PAULA PELL, one of the new writers, said,

Lorne kind of cleaned house on everything and started anew. So it was really great because we all came in together. We also didn't have any idea of how to do the show. None of us had worked on the show before, and since it's such a different beast than anything else, we all had that attitude that "*We're just going to try everything,*" and it was pretty great. It almost felt like going away to college. Everyone was in all these little dorm rooms. In the hall everyone was getting to know each other. We went out all the time. We were all fairly young. Not many people were married or had kids yet. It was sort of one of those times when everyone was on the same wavelength. Creatively it's hard to come in and figure out what it all is. We were just going forward. We were like, "*Screw it,*" and, "*Let's just try.*"

We were all energized because everyone was thrilled to have this job.

HISTORY WAS IN THE MAKING!

In the beginning nobody got good reviews.

But I just thought, *They're wrong. They're just following old press. I don't think they've caught on to the fact that this is a renaissance. Because these people are really talented. They. Do. Characters.*[*]

Then I said to myself, *You know what, I'm not gonna read any of this—because they're wrong. And we're gonna kick ass. This group is gonna soar!*

WE NEVER REALLY HAD any formal training at the show on how to deal with the press, but in general Lorne recommended

---

[*] These are just some of the recurring characters during that period:
The Spartan Cheerleaders—Will and Cheri
Goat Boy and Joe Pesci—Jim Breuer
Mr. Peepers and Mango—Chris Kattan
Rita Delvecchio and Colette Reardon, pill addict—Cheri
Roxbury Guys—Chris and Will
Gerald T-Bone Tibbons—Dave Koechner
Bobby and Marty Culp—Will and Ana
Dog Show—Will and me
Bryan Fuller—Tracy Morgan
Ladies Man—Tim Meadows
Delicious Dish NPR Hosts—Ana and me
Celebrity Jeopardy! Sean Connery—Darrell Hammond
Leg Up: Ann Miller and Debbie Reynolds—Cheri and me
Helen Madden, Licensed Joyologist; Sally O'Malley; Jeannie Darcy; Courtney Love; MKG—me
Goth Talk—Chris Kattan and me
More Cowbell—Will
Bill Brasky—Will, Dave, Mark McKinney, Tim, Ana, Norm Macdonald
Ambiguously Gay Duo—Robert Smigel

never, ever saying anything negative about anyone—and if a cast member did that, he was *not pleased.*

When Will Ferrell, Chris Kattan, and I did a movie together, *A Night at the Roxbury,* the director, Amy Heckerling, thought that it would be a good idea for us to do media training to prepare for our movie press. The studio paid for this very elegant and put-together woman with a silk scarf and French manicure to coach us on how to respond to reporters. She spent a day videotaping us in a hotel suite while we answered questions. Then she replayed the video so we could watch ourselves (horrible—but also so funny) and listen to her critiques:

"Smile more! Be positive!"

When she mock interviewed Will, one of her questions was "Now, Will, tell me, why should I go see *A Night at the Roxbury?*"

Will said, "If you come see this movie, I'll give you a million dollars."

"Stop!" she shouted.

And with the camera tightly focused on his face she scolded him:

"I don't think that's funny. Do *you?*" She shook her head. "That's *not* funny!"

She did not have a sense of humor at all.

ON *SATURDAY NIGHT LIVE,* you have to write your way onto the show. It's nothing like being on a sitcom, where a team of writers is writing *for* actors—unless you're an everyman type, like Phil Hartman, Will Ferrell, Dan Aykroyd, or Chris Parnell. Those guys get written for, because lots of sketches need standard authority figures for the funny characters to play off of: the dad or the cop or a teacher, which fit Phil perfectly. His ability to turn those thankless roles into funny ones is why he got cast in so many of them. Every *SNL* cast usually has one guy who does that. But if you're a character guy—or woman—you gotta think of an idea yourself. On *SNL* you're *vying with* seventeen other people for a spot on the show, and it's competitive.

So you have to think of an idea and then pitch it to the host on Monday. Tuesday night you write until the sun rises. People are working till 6:00 a.m. I always felt like I had to *apologize* to Mike Shoemaker, one of the show's legendary longtime producers, if I stepped out at 4:00 a.m. to go home to sleep.

On Wednesday afternoon everyone meets for the formal read-through to go over all the sketches that have been submitted. Tons of scripts and pencils and everyone piled into this big conference room till you're through reading everything by 5:00 or 6:00 in the evening.

When I was on *SNL*, there was a big table just for the cast. Eighteen of us, plus Lorne. And then seventy or so people around the edges of the room: set designers, hair designers, the director, the musical director, all the writers. It was a packed room. And a huge crew.

The seats were assigned by Lorne. He always put me beside him, with David Spade on my other side. When a sketch you'd submitted for yourself came up, you'd try your best to sell it at the table so it got picked for the show.

But you were limited—because you were *sitting at a table*. So if something was super-physical—like Mary Katherine Gallagher—Lorne could only read the stage directions, like "SHE ENTERS—KNOCKS OVER METAL CHAIR," and he wouldn't know what it *was*. You were performing as much as you *could*—if there was some song in the sketch, you'd get up and sing it—but if the sketch was physical, you were limited by the context, because there just wasn't much room to stand up and show them what you were going to do.

Lorne, the head writers, and the producers selected what was going to go into the show after the table read. If your piece got picked, you were elated. And *you* were the producer of that sketch—working with art directors, costumers, set designers, hair designers. Crews began building the sets Thursday and Friday while you rehearsed.

WITH SO MANY OF my *SNL* colleagues from the Groundlings, on writing night I'd hear them in their offices typing and laughing hysterically as they wrote up their characters. They were like machines—very trained. And I was so frustrated that I would go home and cry. I felt like I was in over my head.

I just thought, *Oh, shit, I didn't do the Groundlings, but I do have characters from my stage show that I know work. But how am I gonna get these characters on the air?* I knew I had all this original material.

THEN I REMEMBER THINKING, *Maybe if I could just find a few people to collaborate with* . . . So I tried to talk to one of the writers about Mary Katherine Gallagher.

I handed him a draft of the sketch so he could read on paper a version of exactly what I had done in my stage show.

He gave me this blank look and said, "Ehh. It just doesn't make *sense*."

"You don't understand," I said. "I have performed this. It definitely works."

"You know why this can't work?" he said. "This is never gonna *work* because . . ." blah, blah, blah, blah.

Okay, I thought. *Next!*

When I'd first started, Adam Sandler told me to talk to Steve Koren. Steve was an NBC page who'd worked his way up to writer. He would secretly slip his own stuff into the batch of official writer jokes for Dennis Miller's "Weekend Update." Dennis just assumed they were all official staff jokes and used a lot of them without ever knowing they were coming from a page. Steve got over a hundred jokes—and two update features—on the air before anybody knew he was a writer.

"Koren's a good guy," Adam said.

I found him and asked, "Could you help me write a sketch?"

He said, "Sure. I'll help you."

I showed him a picture of Mary Katherine from my show. "*Here's* the character."

He laughed. "All right. Well, let's write her."

We sat down right there in his office and worked all night long writing the very first Mary Katherine Gallagher sketch. We decided to have her be a Catholic schoolgirl auditioning for a talent show. I told Steve exactly what I did in my stage show. Then he buoyed it with a few more solid jokes that I could land on, and we typed up our first sketch together and were done.

What Steve remembered was "You did the fully developed character in my office and I was blown away and felt it was my job to just come up with a setting and organize the sketch for TV with jokes, and you could enter as the character and destroy."

We submitted it to table read and Lorne said, "I really like that character, so we're gonna save it for next week and put it in the Gabriel Byrne show."

Lorne liked Catholic stuff and, I think, really saw the potential. And he knew Gabriel Byrne would make a good priest. And Gabriel had an Irish brogue like Father Murray, the priest who had been so kind and truthful to me after my mom, Katie, and Fran died.

JUST GETTING A SKETCH *picked* was a really big deal. We'd cast Will, Jim Breuer, and Cheri when we were writing it. Then everyone arrived at 1:00 p.m. on Saturday, the show day, for a run-through/dress rehearsal. This led up to the 8:00 p.m. taped dress show before the official live broadcast at 11:30 p.m.

I would always stop in the little coffee shop in the lobby of 30 Rock and get a fried egg sandwich with American cheese, salt, pepper, and mayonnaise on white toast with a bag of barbecue potato chips—yum!—before going up to my dressing room on the ninth floor.

For the dress, they did a fatter show, putting in sketches—maybe four extra—that would probably get cut. A lot of the time stuff they didn't believe in would be low in the dress show schedule. They wanted to test everything out with an audience before the live show to see what was going to work. You rehearsed all day Saturday. If they got to dinner break (5:00 p.m.) and you didn't get to rehearse one of your sketches, they probably didn't really believe in it.

And that's what happened with Mary Katherine. We didn't even get to rehearse. They ran out of time—because it was *way* at the bottom. Before it was our turn, they were just calling out, "That's it! Dinner!"

We ended up talking it out really quickly during the dinner break, no formal blocking on camera. I was so mad. I thought, *They're not understanding. I must not have really performed it enough at the read-through. I don't know if they understand, physically, what this is. So I'm gonna really have to show them, because I don't think they get it.*

Then, based on how stuff played during the dress show, they switched the whole order up: "Oh, this was really hot. . . . That sketch tanked. Let's cut it. . . ."

I thought, *I'm gonna have to fucking blow the roof off.*

DURING THE EIGHT O'CLOCK dress show I remember being backstage right before I went on—and it's a full audience. They counted you down before you went out. The stage manager, Gena Rositano, was saying, "Five, four, three, two, one, go!" My heart was pounding. *Ga-dunk! Ga-dunk! Ga-dunk!* I really wanted a chance to be like the boys, like Chris Farley, and be *physical.*

I gotta show them, I thought. And I decided to use my *actual* nervousness: *It is amazing that I, Molly Shannon, am so fucking scared that I am getting to do this on* SNL—*but I can pour my own nervousness into the character.*

So when Gabriel Byrne said, "Yes, and the next auditioner is . . ." I came in guns blazing.

I went wild.

At the end of the sketch, after shouting, "I can do gymnastics, Father! Back flip! Back flip! Back flip! Back flip!" I *sailed* backwards, crashing into a stack of folding chairs, with no padding—all metal chairs. And people started screaming. The audience went fucking nuts. I got cheers.

Jim Breuer said he'd never heard the audience scream that loud. He said, "It was like a roar."

Fred Wolf the head writer, said, "Oh my God, nobody could believe it. Everyone was like *Holy shit!*'"

During my dress performance Lorne had been talking with him under the bleachers where the audience sat but stopped midsentence to see what was happening. Laughter got his attention. He suddenly realized that it was not just some little character sketch. He realized it was more than that—that I was killing. So he put on his headphones and suddenly had laser focus. He realized he had a hit and started giving Steve Koren notes.

BETWEEN DRESS AND AIR, we all piled into Lorne's office, where there was a bulletin board covered in little index cards. We all walked in nervously and looked at the board to see what had gotten cut and what had made it into the live show.

And my sketch had gone from the *bottom* of the show to the *top*.

I thought, *Yes! Now we're talking, baby!*

FRED WOLF TOLD ME LATER, "I often cite your MKG sketch as a great example of how comedy can be different in the mind's eye versus on its feet with a great performer. . . . Luckily, Lorne carried the day.

"My exact words to him after your dress MKG: 'Jesus, you were right: it's top of the show. Please tell me you made a mistake like this once?'

"He says he did, but I think he's just being polite."

THEN, RIGHT BEFORE AIR—like 11:17 for the 11:30 show—Lorne rushed into the hair-and-makeup room, something he *never* did, and said, "I think your skirt should be *shorter*—so that when you lift your leg up onto the stool, it'll be funny. It should be really short."

I thought back to the woman who wasn't so interested in women telling me, "Lorne Michaels is never going to like that dirty little character."

Turns out Lorne Michaels *loved* that dirty little schoolgirl. He said, "I want her."

RIGHT BEFORE THE LIVE SHOW, I asked Steve Koren, "Where should I look while I'm out there?"

"Just play as much as possible *straight to camera*," he told me.

"*Okay. Okay. Got it, got it!*"

And that's what I did.

When the sketch was over and Gabriel Byrne was sitting onstage with his head in his hands, I jumped back in for one last lunge. It wasn't scripted. I just wanted to make Debbie Palermo laugh. It was a private joke just for her. I knew she was watching out in LA.

So I jumped back in and said, "*Superstar!*"

I just sort of muttered it under my breath. I wanted to make her happy. And it blew her mind. She'd known me as a *kid* and I'd said our little joke.

MARY KATHERINE WANTS TO be a star and she wants to be seen and she wants her mom to come back from the dead. My dad is the grandmother character: "Go to New York City. Use your singing voice. You look like a young Elizabeth

Taylor." She's shy, shy, shy till she gains confidence; then she's so bad, she gets sent away. I just exaggerated everything I felt.

And there's something so freeing about doing a character and not thinking about how you look. I didn't want to look pretty. I wanted to look like the character. I wanted to have no makeup, headband, white face—plain Jane.

The sketch is a story of somebody who against all odds succeeds. The character is a survivor. She struggles to rise above the wreckage. A girl who trips. Who breaks things. Who's nervous. Who's in her head. Who obsesses. Gets crushes. Fucks up. But gets back up.

It's an emotional character. I wrote from my heart.

AFTER I DID MARY KATHERINE that first time, so many people came up to me on the street and at the show. One of the cameramen said, "My sister saw that. She loved it! She said she's the same way!" Later I would get thousands of photographs from gay men, women of all ages, little girls, all dressed up as Mary Katherine Gallagher. This happened with all my characters, but that was the beginning. It was crazy.

It was such a great lesson to really write from your heart—from yourself—what's true, not reacting to boys, just being a girl and being yourself and writing from your heart. It blew my mind *how many people* responded to it.

It came from *within*.

CHAPTER 15

Team Shannon

THE STUNTMEN SAID, "SHE'S FUCKING OUT OF HER MIND." They couldn't believe I would just leap backwards and fall on top of a bunch of metal chairs.

I didn't use any padding. I didn't even think of it. I just fell into the metal chairs without anything to protect me.

Steve Koren said, "You threw yourself into those chairs more forcefully than anyone predicted and I was shocked and the audience screamed and after that I made sure everything was padded because I knew you'd commit one hundred percent and possibly injure yourself."

But I liked being roughed up. And when I was performing the character, I was so in the moment that I couldn't feel anything. I woke up Sunday morning, bruised and cut, muscles aching—but it felt so good because I had poured my fucking body into what I was doing. I liked how it felt.

It felt really good.

Until so many people started to ask me, "Do you ever get hurt?" Then it started to freak me out.

I'm so grateful that I'm okay. I never broke my neck or hurt my back.

I did do a lot of stretching before I would perform.

WHEN THEY REALIZED WHAT Mary Katherine Gallagher was, and that the character was going to be a hit, they hired a new stunt coordinator, Brian Smyj.

A friend of his at NBC called him up and said, "Hey, Brian, go down and take over the show, because they've got a new cast member. They've got the new Chris Farley there. And she's gonna need a lot of attention."

Brian was this big, protective guy—half Irish and half Russian. (He'd say about his parents, "I don't know how those two got along well enough to have three kids.") As soon as he came on, I felt taken care of and could just relax and have fun.

Brian; Deb Weber, my dresser; and Theresa Hayde, the set med nurse, called themselves "Team Shannon."

Brian said, "Our goal was to keep you in one piece and to protect Molly Shannon from Mary Katherine Gallagher. You were a meal ticket for everyone. OMG, I was worried about you getting hurt in any capacity. You were the crown jewel."

Kenny Aymong—*SNL*'s brilliant supervising producer and Lorne's right-hand guy—used that crown jewel term all the time after the first MKG sketch. He'd tell Brian, the stuntman, "She's our show. Keep the crown jewel intact."

Brian always had to be thinking, *What's the worst that could happen? How do we protect her from that?*

I always would tell him before performing, "Don't worry, I'm not gonna go *that* far."

And he would just think, *Molly is telling me she's not gonna go that far, but when MKG shows up, she's a hurricane and she's not gonna agree to any of Molly's rules!*

"Your alter ego scared the hell out of us," he told me. "I was terrified all the time. I could talk to *Molly,* but when MKG went on set, you walked right past me. You helped me understand the whole idea of *becoming the character.*"

AND WHEN I WOULD come offstage after performing, Brian remembers that Deb and Theresa would be watching the monitor.

"Theresa would put her hand on my arm and ask about you, 'She okay?'

"Yeah, she's okay."

"Okay, I'll check her out."

Deb had a very dry sense of humor. "Looks great to me," she'd say. Then she'd turn to Brian and Theresa and add, "We dodged another one."

Deb really understood me and what it had been like to be raised without a mother. She used to dip my MKG schoolgirl blouse in tea so I had a dirty collar. And she would dirty up my Carterettes underwear so it looked like a man did my laundry—not a woman. Like I wasn't really being looked after properly.

THAT FIRST YEAR STEVE KOREN wrote a Mary Katherine Gallagher sketch that's one of Lorne's favorites. Mine, too. St. Monica's is doing a high school production of *West Side Story*—and we got to use the real music, though NBC can never replay it because the rights are too steep, which makes me love it all the more. (I wanted it on my Best-of tape but it was too expensive.)

I played the prop girl. Will and Teri Hatcher played Tony and Maria.

Maria starts singing "One Hand, One Heart" while Mary Katherine stands in the background. But after Maria sings for maybe thirty seconds, Mary Katherine just shoves her out of the way and takes her place so that she can kiss Tony/Will.

It's drama mixed with comedy and love. And I think that combination is what Lorne likes best.

THEN WHEN GWYNETH PALTROW hosted we did a Mary Katherine Gallagher sketch together with Cheri and Ana, about a bad girls gang at St. Monica's, with Gwyneth playing the main bad girl. Before the sketch, Brian Smyj told Gwyneth, "MKG and Molly Shannon are not the same person." Just so she'd be prepared for me to go crazy. But she did not fully comprehend what he was saying.

For that sketch, the designers built this bathroom set with three foam core walls, real toilets, a couple sinks, and a metal tampon dispenser. Since the set was on center stage, the band was behind the back wall.

Brian told the set designers, "Hey, those toilets gotta go."

He knew those walls were going down and I could easily crack my head on the toilets as I crashed through backwards.

"She said she's not gonna knock down the wall," they replied.

But Brian told them, "*Molly* said *she's* not gonna knock down the wall. But *MKG's* not gonna tell us *what* she's gonna do."

Of course, I knocked down all three of the stall walls during the live show. I would've taken down the back wall, too, if Richie from special effects and Brian hadn't been holding it up. Lenny Pickett, *SNL's* musical director, ran over with his sax to help hold up that wall with one hand. "You were like a hurricane," Brian said. Then I kicked the tampon dispenser off the wall.

Kenny Aymong came up to Brian afterward and asked, "When did you get a breakaway tampon dispenser?"

"It *wasn't* breakaway," he said. "It's metal. She just kicked it off the wall."

Kenny said, "Who does she think she is, Bruce Lee?"

ANOTHER TIME THERE WAS a railing on set that wasn't break-away.

Brian told the design department, "This railing here. It's gotta go."

They said, "No, no, no—it's gonna be fine. She won't go near that."

He said, "Molly is gonna hit that railing."

But they didn't want to move it.

So *Brian* ripped it off the wall. He just broke it off and said, "*Now* we're not using it."

He told me later, "I got in this big argument. Big pissing match," until Kenny Aymong came out and asked Brian what was going on and Brian said, "Kenny, I'm doing my job. I'm here to protect Molly. I told them it doesn't work and it's dangerous. They wouldn't remove it—so I removed it. I removed a dangerous situation."

In our design department's defense, they truly thought I would not go near that railing—but Brian knew better.

BRIAN LIKED TO SAY about stuntwomen: "Ginger Rogers did everything Fred Astaire did—backwards and in six-inch heels."

"And what you did with that character," he told me, "was become a stuntperson. You did the physical comedy like Chris Farley. But Chris could wear all this *stuff.* And he was a big guy. He had the natural padding. So he was protected. But you had the little tiny frame on you. There were stuntwomen that were *horrified* because when they did falls, the director would use you as an example for what they wanted to see the stuntwomen do. When you're a stuntperson, they'll show you what an actor did or does on a regular basis and you can't then do *less*. You can't even do exactly what the actor does and get away with it. You have to do *more*! You set a benchmark for stunts."

WHEN I FIRST STARTED ON *SNL*, Adam Sandler told me this: "Soon people are gonna know your name. They'll call out, 'Molly!'"

Really? I thought. *They will? That is so cool!*

Now it had happened. People knew my name. Tons of people. They would come up to me on the streets of New York City and LA and say, "Hey, Molly!"

But as good as it felt, I still had this anxious, sad longing. They would say such nice things, but it was not fully satisfying.

The one person I wanted more than anyone to tell me I was good was my mom. She was really the only one I wanted. I had thought if I could just be good enough, funny enough—do back flips and make everyone laugh and cheer—then maybe she would come back. But all this and she was still not coming back.

At that point I got depressed for a bunch of months. I finally let myself be fully, deeply sad. I couldn't escape it. The longing had kept me connected to my mom since she'd died. I realized I'd been running for years, driven to work so hard, on this track, trying to make it, to *achieve*, and when I finally got there . . . there was still that *ache*. But it was a relief to realize fame doesn't fix anything—including having to pay back your student loans: busted. It was a profound revelation.

And then I completely changed my whole philosophy. After that, I could just enjoy being creative. It didn't matter if I was number one or number four thousand. I didn't have to be the best. It was a relief.

My hairstylist Clariss Morgan said, "You can't buy an education like this," and it suddenly hit me how to look at the experience.

I decided to treat the show as a creative-arts comedy camp. A writing and performing boot camp—the best one imaginable.

And if I wasn't on the show one week, I tried to think, *Oh, whatever, let me just try to enjoy it as an artistic experience. Look at the training I'm getting. I'm surrounded by all these amazing writers. This is like the Harvard of comedy. I'm getting written for and I'm getting to perform my own writing.*

I had that positive attitude so I wouldn't be so result oriented or disappointed if I wasn't in the show. I always felt if a sketch didn't get picked, it was usually because it wasn't good enough. I didn't take it personally. And with all the competition, you can't second-guess what sketches are gonna make it to air anyhow.

Robert Smigel used to remind me that if you weren't in the show for a week, you were like a baseball player who was benched for a game. It's hard, but it's a long season. It's up and down.

He always said, "Don't think in terms of 'Oh, I wasn't in that *one* show.' Nobody's gonna look at it that way. So don't be hard on yourself that way. Think about the season as a whole. People will remember the overall body of work."

ONCE ANA GASTEYER JOINED the cast, she, Cheri, and I would become a trifecta. It was a big change, because there hadn't been strong women at the center of the show for a little while.

Ana said, "I think we were exalted, for reasons that weren't always clear to me early on, Molly Shannon and Cheri Oteri and I. We got press for it. We got press for being this trifecta of women that turned the show around. I mean, that's what they talked about. . . . [W]e were written up and we were photographed together. That sort of signifies that you've changed a tune, and certainly we heard it anecdotally all the time— that the women are the best thing on the show."[*]

ONE MONDAY NIGHT I didn't have any ideas, so I just blurted out, "I'm going to do *The Courtney Love Show*."

It was a fake pitch. But then Lorne had Mike Shoemaker call me at home on Thursday night and say, "Hey, can we have *The Courtney Love Show*? We need it for the show. Can you write it up?"

If it had been a real pitch, I would have worked on it Tuesday.

Steve Koren and I had to crank it out really quickly.

The super-talented costume designers who created all the looks for the characters, Tom Broecker, Dale Richards, Eric Justian—and wardrobe supervisor Donna Richards, Dale's sister—put me in a thin white satin dress with bright red lipstick. As Courtney, I smoked all the time, made out with guests, made out with the camera guys, surprised the stage manager by grabbing and kissing him—and couldn't hold on

---

[*] Tom Shales and Andrew J. Miller, *Live from New York: The Complete, Uncensored History of Saturday Night Live as Told by Its Stars, Writers, and Guests* (Little, Brown and Company, 2002).

to any thought or question for more than a few seconds. And it just went really well. I loved performing her, because she was my total opposite. I was the good girl. She was the bad girl. I never wanted to make anyone feel left out. She didn't give a shit.

The Courtney Love Show was on a few different times. It was a blast.

But then Courtney herself showed up one Saturday night when I was doing her in a sketch.

This was while she was in preproduction and about to shoot *The People vs. Larry Flynt*. She was stone-cold sober.

Someone told me, "Courtney Love is here, in the building, and she is *hunting you down*."

She was roaming around during the live broadcast shouting, "Where's *Molly*!? I'm gonna *kick her ass*."

The second I heard that I thought, *Oh, no. I hope she's not gonna punch me out.* I was petrified.

And then she found me. I was face-to-face with a statuesque girl who smelled like witchy oils. And I'm dressed as her.

I thought, *Wow, she's really tall.*

She said, "Are you making fun of me?"

But before she could do anything else, I said, "Can you gimme a cigarette?"

It caught her by surprise.

"Oh . . . sure."

I flipped it on her. After which she ended up being sweet.

As we smoked I told her, "I'm a big fan of yours. And the impression is a form of flattery."

I really was a giant fan. I went to see her in concert at the Hollywood Palace with my friend Mike Rad when we waited tables together at Mel 'n' Rose's, after Cravings.

But I was also scared.

EVERYONE ALWAYS WANTED TICKETS to the show. Every week I had friends in the audience who were excited to see *me*. And after the live broadcast, in the big black stretch limo on the way to the after-party—each cast member had their *own* stretch limo to go to the party every Saturday night—if I had not been in the show much, they would say, "*More Molly!* We wanted *more Molly*! Why isn't there *more Molly*?" And I'd be so hard on myself.

I got to a point early on where I would only invite friends who knew the way it worked, how hard it was to get on air, who understood the rules, who were supportive. That way, when we went to the party after the show, they wouldn't give me the whole "More Molly!" thing and make me feel bad.

Because the danger was that I might start thinking, *Oh. My. God. I've made it this far and it still isn't enough.*

I started to be careful about who I invited. Of course, it was thrilling when I was in a sketch that people loved and we'd go out to celebrate and stay out till the sun came up. We'd all be on cloud nine, with so much adrenaline and energy, the party just starting at 1:30 in the morning.

WHENEVER ANYONE TALKED ABOUT *SNL* as a launching pad or stepping-stone for careers, I just thought, *Stepping-stone?! That is ridiculous!*

This is the island where I want to camp for life. This is just the greatest. There will be no job like this ever again. Baby, this is it! I really appreciated the job because I'd hustled so hard to get it.

It *exceeded* all my expectations. I always thought I would have been happy just being a waitress, serving hot biscuits, coffee, and sizzling sausage on red-and-white checkered tablecloths at a Bob Evans restaurant.

Being a waitress *was* a job I thought I could've done and had a good, simple, happy life.

"Morning, everybody! Got the coffee on!"

I THINK LORNE APPRECIATED that I thought about *SNL* that way. I really knew what it was and I knew the power of television. There wasn't somewhere I was looking to go from there. I just thought, *This is a unique job in television. It's a live television show. It's one-of-a-kind. Lorne Michaels is a legend. There's nobody like him in show business. Not even close.* I really realized what it was.

I thought, *This is the pinnacle of everything. This live variety performance experience is probably going to be the greatest of all.* And Lorne's whole world was so separate from Hollywood. I liked *his* world. And it was a world that was wonderful to women. That was certainly my experience.

I was working with people who became some of the biggest power players in show business. To this day. Some of the biggest producers, writers, and show runners. At that time, they were all unknowns, all up-and-coming, which is why I believe so strongly that you need to build your relationships with the people you click with.

CINDY CAPONERA WAS ONE of the *SNL* writers I really liked working with. She had been reading a catalogue from the Learning Annex, trying to find inspiration, and came across a woman advertising herself as a "joyologist" in the back section.

She said, "It was crazy to me that someone would consider herself an expert in joy. I couldn't imagine what she would be like, but anything that sounded *that* insane would have to be hilarious."

Cindy and I wrote the character together: Helen Madden, Licensed Joyologist. I used parts of my dad's personality in creating her—the way he could get into a super-excited, happy mood—and mixed that with the character.

I improvised a lot, and it got to the point that Cindy knew she had to keep a sketch short because of what I was going to add once I got in front of the audience. She had to imagine how physical I'd get and the unexpected things that might happen as a result. One time I was kicking so hard in a sketch with Matthew Broderick, playing my seashell craftsman boyfriend, I accidentally went over backwards in my chair. The crowd loved it.

MY DAD ALSO LOVED strong female performers, and I wanted to become one of the types he admired. Elizabeth Taylor. Rosalind Russell. Judy Garland. Strong dames.

Cheri Oteri and I had a sketch that we wrote with Steve Koren called "Leg Up" where I played Ann Miller, and Cheri played Debbie Reynolds. We wore red sequined leotards cut high on the thigh and suggestively crossed/uncrossed/recrossed our legs while making salacious remarks.

"Just watching Gene Kelly *slide* into his tights used to put dew on my lily."

Right after we started, the *New York Times* published a picture of us on the front page of the arts section. Cheri and I also appeared in the *Daily News*, and the TV critic Eric Mink singled out, "fresh, even daring, comic thinking at work and the willingness to take chances." It felt like women were suddenly at the center of the show again. It had been a boys' club for a while, and a very funny one, but women had taken a back seat. These articles marked a sea change for women. Suddenly our sketches started being at the top of the show again.

And as he kept watching, Eric Mink at the *Daily News* observed, "The numerous characters created during the season by Will, Molly, David Koechner, Cheri, and Mark McKinney all say and do funny things and at the same time manage to be human and vulnerable. That's a rare and precious combination in comedy."

A LOT OF THE characters I developed were impressions of my father—versions of my father but disguised as women.

I really wanted to get my original character Sally O'Malley from my stage show on *SNL* and was trying to figure out how to do it. Then Lori Nasso, one of our many incredible female writers, met this woman at the Equinox gym on the Upper West Side. She was giving Lori a tour, trying to get her to become a member, and kept emphasizing what great shape she was in—and that she was fifty.

She threw her arms in the air and said, "I'm *fifty*—and *this is what fifty should look like!*"

So Lori wrote this sketch up for me based on that woman. It made it to the read-through a couple of times but never got picked. Then, when a great writer named Jerry Collins joined *SNL* in 1998 (now he's Lori's husband!), he thought we should have Sally O'Malley from my stage show, combined with Lori's gym lady, do a tryout for the Rockettes.

We put the ideas together when Danny DeVito was the host and cast him as the choreographer/auditioner. Jerry Collins and Paula Pell and I worked on the sketch, and Lorne loved the idea.

The character Sally O'Malley was a response to my dad's physical limitations. Because of how much I wished my dad could walk faster when I was little, and move the way he could before the accident, a lot of the characters I do really show a physical strength. They are breaking out.

In her first *SNL* appearance, Sally O'Malley comes on limping while she walks and introduces herself: "Ladies and gentlemen my name is Sally O'Malley." That's my dad's limp after the accident. Just how my dad walks. "I'm proud to say I'm fifty years old. I'm not one of those gals who's afraid to tell her real age."

And then *Bam!*—"And I like to kick, stretch, and *kiiick!* I'm fifty! Fifty years old!"

It's a surprise. That surprise big kick is me wishing my dad could kick those braces off his legs. As in: *Don't be fooled by the limp, because I'm a motherfucker.*

He can blow the braces off his legs and fuck you all up. He's a powerhouse.

I don't know if it was anger. I know it was physical and it felt good!

CHAPTER 16

Studio 8H

I F YOU WANTED TO GET THE WEEK'S HOST TO BE IN YOUR sketch, you had to pitch them an idea in the Monday meeting. And if they were on board, then you'd go write it up.

When Jennifer Aniston hosted *SNL*, I never told her I had seen her at Cravings. She was in a sketch with Sting and me, and she was a pro. So easygoing and fun and game for anything. The best hosts are the ones who are open and willing to do anything and just go with the flow. The hosts who trust Lorne and the writers. Lorne and the producers always want to make the hosts look good. Jim Carrey was another one who just came on and would try anything—elevating every sketch he was in with ideas. And I had waited on him, too.

Alec Baldwin was the best. He was always game for anything. Once when he was hosting, a bunch of us went out for dinner—Alec, Will, Cheri, Chris Kattan—and I said, "Let's play truth or dare!"

He said, "Let's *do it*."

So I said, "Alec I *dare* you to go back into the kitchen, unbutton your shirt, show your big hairy chest, and ask the kitchen staff, in your sexiest voice, 'Do you have any more *red hot pepper?*'"

And he *did* it. He went back there and ripped it open.

I mean he *really opened it*—and *delivered* that line.

We were all in hysterics.

MUSICAL GUESTS DIDN'T COME to rehearse till Thursday, so the cast wasn't really interacting with them. They just came in the afternoon, sound checked, did their songs, and then left. And then they came back Saturday for the dress show. So people in the cast didn't always think to go talk to the bands that came on *SNL*. But once in a while some band members would ask to be in a sketch or get invited to be in a sketch.

Tim Herlihy came up with an idea when Steven Tyler and Aerosmith were on the show. Mike Myers was hosting and Tim and another writer, my good friend Matt Piedmont, wrote the band into a Mary Katherine Gallagher sketch.

The premise was that I was supposed to be a superfan auditioning to star in their next music video. I'd go absolutely wild as they played "Sweet Emotion" and crash through this brick wall at the end, overwhelmed with excitement.

Brian Smyj, my stunt guy, told me, "It was terrifying. Theresa and Deb came to me and said, 'Oh, we are in trouble. Aerosmith is here. She loves Aerosmith.'"

Brian shook his head and said, "Oh, boy. We're going to DEFCON 1."

SO THEN I'M OUT there with Steven Tyler—he's shirtless, in these tight pants—and I start to get lost in the moment. When he sang "stand in the front just a shakin' your ass!" I got down on the ground and started licking him. I licked him like I was unable to resist as he sang out "Sweeeeeeeeeet Eeeeemoooootion!"—and then pretended to snap out of it and act shocked at myself and my hidden desires.

Like a nerdy teenage girl who has a hungry tiger inside of her . . . and then comes to and can't *believe* herself: *OH MY! I didn't know I had that in me*!

And everyone loved it—except for the NBC lawyer.

She came up after the dress and said, "You *absolutely* cannot do that in the live show. *Okay? Stay above the belt* for censors."

I said, "Okay. Sure. Sure."

Then, for the live show, the brick wall I'd crashed through wasn't ready. The brick wall was actually balsa wood painted to look like brick, and Brian and his crew would cut the wood beforehand so you could break through it fairly easily. But they didn't have enough time to stack the fake balsa wood bricks and the sketch was about to start and I thought, *Oh, no, the wall I'm supposed to break through is not ready. What am I gonna do? Oh God, the whole sketch leads up to this. . . . Oh, no.* There I was, backstage, getting counted down, about to go on, panicked, "Five . . . four . . . three . . . two . . . ," and saying to myself, *Shit, shit, shit, shit, shit.*

In moments like that, Lorne would always appear suddenly and let you know with his eyes that everything would be okay. Now he was across from me on the other side of the stage and noticing how worried I was.

He gave me this reassuring look that said, *Don't let it throw you off. Look at me. Just do it. Don't let this goof you up. Don't worry about the wall. You're gonna be fine, Molly.*

And I nodded back and went onstage.

Lorne's encouragement fueled my performance. I really

committed. Brian said, "You were like a tornado. I was stand-ing off the stage, spotting you. If they replay it, you can see me standing there. I look like a roadie. You went through the chairs and I actually caught you when you came flying off the stage and put you right back on the stage. I'm dying. I'm pissing myself."

And then when it came time to lick Steven Tyler, I just thought, *Aw, fuck it,* dropped down to the ground, and ran my tongue all the way up his body, from his toes to the top of his head—on live television. I went W-I-L-D. And he really played along and was so fun to perform with.

He loved every second of it.

And the lawyer never made another sound.

CONAN O'BRIEN ONCE SAID something that I really agree with: "Comedy is like music. The rhythm of comedy is connected to the rhythm of music. They're both about creating tension and knowing when to let it go. I'm always surprised when somebody funny is not musical."

And after the Aerosmith sketch I started realizing, *Oh, these rock stars want to talk to cast members. And they're so excited to meet us. These musicians really want to perform in sketches. They understand comedy on a visceral level.*

This is intriguing.

I decided to act like I was the ambassador and it was my show. I was going to go introduce myself to every lead singer in every band. And the band members if I could.

So I went up to Bono, Tina Turner, Whitney Houston, and said, "Hi, I'm Molly, and I just wanna say we're so ex-cited to have you on the show"—acting like I was the hostess of the show, welcoming them.

And they all seemed to appreciate it. Most of them were fans of *SNL,* naturally funny, and knew the show well.

They'd say, "Thank *you* so much, Molly! We're so happy to be here!"

I'd already been on the show for a while at this point and I thought, *Oh my God, I wish I had done this the entire time, because I could have met every band.* But once I figured it out, I really made it a habit to *always* go introduce myself.

Bono was the most charismatic. There was this parting of the waters when he was around. An electric presence. And he was kind and supportive. He came up after one of my sketches and said, "Molly, that was *great!*"

I thought, *B O N O !*

And when he sang, he blew the roof off the house.

THE HOST ONE WEEK was Rosie O'Donnell. I adore Rosie. She's Irish like me and lost her mom when she was ten years old—we bonded over it. So I asked her to play the Mother Superior at Mary Katherine Gallagher's parochial school, St. Monica's. In the sketch, we're putting on the Christmas school spectacular, and since Whitney Houston was the musical guest, I thought, *We should get her in the sketch, too!*

But everyone said, "Whitney's never gonna be in a sketch. She doesn't even show up. She's going to be twelve hours late. Don't waste your time. She'll never do it."

I said, "Actually, I think she will."

Then I thought, *If I were her, what would I want? If I wasn't in the mood to memorize all these lines or have extra work?*

And I realized, *I'll just make it super-fun for her. She's a singer. Don't give her pages of dialogue to bog her down. She's Whitney Houston. She's in New York City. She likes to party.*

She just wants to be free and have fun and not have to memorize a bunch of lines.

Writers can sometimes make it too hard for the musical guests who aren't actors, giving them too much dialogue. I figured out a way to make it appealing.

I went up to her and said, "Okay, so this is what it's gonna be. You and I are gonna sing 'Little Drummer Boy' and all I need for you to do is out-sing me. Do whatever you want. Say whatever you want. Push me out of the way. Stick your tongue out at me. You're the *snotty* schoolgirl"—I could tell she liked that—"it will be easy." She was nodding enthusiastically.

Then she clapped her hands and said, "Yeah, yeah. Okay. *I'll do it*! Yeah!"

But then—*yikes!*—she had not yet shown up Saturday night, and my sketch was at the top of the show, right after the monologue. Ana Gasteyer had to get the Catholic uniform costume on just in case Whitney wasn't going to make it. (Of course, Ana would have killed in the part, but it was a big deal to have gotten Whitney to agree to be in the sketch.)

I thought, *She's going to show up. I know she's going to show up. I made it so fun. She's just going to turn up at the very last second.*

It was the big sketch. The feature sketch. The rest of us were *actually onstage* seconds away from starting. But Whitney still hadn't shown.

THEN, *LITERALLY FIVE SECONDS* before Ana was about to go on, all dressed and ready to do Whitney's part, Whitney appeared like a vision.

"Oh my God, Whitney's here—*swap them!*"

I thought, *Yes!*

And Whitney *delivered*. She was fantastic. It's now a famous sketch that they replay all the time at Christmas.

After the show, in the hallways of Studio 8H, with all these fans surrounding her, Whitney spotted me and, with the biggest smile on her face, said, "Girl—you are so *crazy*! That was so *fun*!"

She was so happy and excited and sweet, and I could tell she had a good silly sense of humor. Silly—I knew that.

SNL WOULD ORDER DINNER for all of us from different restaurants and all the writers would obsess about whether it should be sushi, or Chinese, or Mexican, and when the food came they would all hang around the food table—to *avoid writing*.

It was all about using food to avoid writing.

Paula Pell was one of my favorite writers and performers. She would laugh so much on writing nights because I would always change my mind about what I thought of something in the middle of a bite.

"This is you, Molly," she'd say, imitating me: "'Mmmm, this chicken soup is delish—*disgusting!*'"

I didn't realize—and then it made me laugh so much.

She was one of the premier writers who everyone wanted to work with, so you had to nail her down to get a time to work with her. She was in high demand. I collaborated with her on some of my favorite sketches and characters. We would laugh and talk about relationships and family—having the best time till the sun rose.

After read-throughs, on Wednesdays, Adam McKay, Dennis McNicholas, Chris Kattan, Matt Piedmont, Will Ferrell,

Harper Steele, Tim Meadows, and Paula and I would all go out for drinks at McSorley's to unwind, and celebrate if our sketches got picked.

AT *SNL* IT WAS great if you found a performer you could really sit down and write with. For me that person was Will. I was just very comfortable writing with him. We have the same sense of humor. I felt like I could be myself when we wrote together.

Together, Will and I wrote a very silly sketch called "Dog Show." My character was Miss Coleen and Will was my husband, Mr. David Larry. We were obsessed with our dogs, Mr. Rocky Balboa and Mr. Bojangles. ("Mr. Bojangles is really a girl!" Will said, "but I'm playing a trick on her.")

But I was also mad that Mr. David Larry was gay. I couldn't stop talking about our relationship problems.

> **ME:** "Sometimes I think our love is dead because you like *men*, Mr. David Larry."
>
> **WILL:** "Maybe I do and maybe I *do*."

We all had so much fun making up insane dog names together: Lord Pistachio, Sugar Breath, Little Mr. Miami Beach, Captain Gingersnap.

Will also *knew* that he could make me laugh. In a sketch that Matt Murray and Chris Kattan wrote, I'm on a date with Charlie Sheen at a TGI Fridays. Will comes in and introduces himself as "*Thaddeus Garfield Ignatius Friday . . .* world famous railroad tycooooon and oooowner of *This Fine Establishment!*"

Everyone in the sketch started to laugh. We couldn't control ourselves. It was so hard to keep a straight face. Because Will was doing it on purpose—trying to make us laugh.

Charlie was complaining about the service, so Will asked, "Would a complimentary Brownie Caesar Salad change your mind?" And then he screamed, "Brooowwwwnie Saaalll-laaads fooorrr *EEEVVVVEEERRRRYYYYOOOONNNNE EEE!*"

We were dying. All of us.

Sometimes I could hardly perform in a sketch with Will because I would just start laughing. And I think it's a good sign when someone laughs during a sketch. It shows that you're open, you're really listening, and *your instrument* is *relaxed*. The audience likes it, too. It gives *them* license to laugh. And they feel in on something happening live.

One time Will and I were in a sketch with Brendan Fraser where I played Xena the Warrior Princess and Brendan played a rival warrior princess. Ana, Tim Meadows, Jim Breuer, and Chris Kattan were in it, too. It was a big cast. And I was supposed to grab Brendan's Viking hat. But I accidentally grabbed and pulled off his wig—just removed his whole wig. He had a wig cap on beneath it. My first thought was, *Okay, can we stop for a second? Because we have to put this wig back on.*

And then I remembered, *Oh my God, this is live television. We. Can't. Stop.*

And we all broke character and laughed so hard. We were in hysterics, all of us, we just broke down and could not stop laughing through the whole sketch—it was so much fun.

ONE OF MY FAVORITE sketches I did with Will was based on something that happened to me. There was this really pretty actress from Texas, Samantha Travis, who got on one of those big soap operas when we were in drama school.

And when she got cast I thought, *Ooh, I would love to get cast on a soap opera.*

But then she turned it down and ended up not acting at all.

Once, when she was visiting LA, I stopped by the apartment where she was staying. She had brought these photo albums from New York and laid them all out.

I said, "Oh, can I see those?"

And she replied, "No. I'm sorry. No."

It was a mysterious boundary. I thought, *I can't? Oooh!* It made me want to look at them *more.*

When I told Will that story he thought it was hilarious. Just "*No. No.*" Without explanation.

It made *us* laugh, so Will and I wrote a sketch about a couple meeting for a blind date at an airport bar.

When I travel I like to study people waiting for their planes at airport bars. I think about their lives. *Where are they headed?* I wonder. *How long is their layover? Oh, interesting, he's drinking a Heineken. It's only noon.*

In the sketch Will asks my character some innocent question and I reply, just like my soap opera friend, "You know what, I don't really want to talk about that right now. I just met you and I don't know you all that well. . . ."

I set a mysterious boundary and just *shut the conversation down.*

Writers in particular loved that sketch. The audience didn't know what to think. There were no standard jokes. It was too real. They just thought we were improvising. The sketch was about two lonely people looking for love who *almost* connect. You're rooting for them but they are not a match.

There was this sweet moment after I'd shut him down when Will said, "I sell eyeglasses. I know it sounds weird."

"It doesn't sound weird," I said.

"Oh, good, yeah."

"I think it's so cute when you see little babies or little children that wear little glasses. It's *so* cute!"

"*Yes!* Or babies that wear sunglasses!"

"Exactly!"

"Adorable, it really is."

And then I said, "You know what, I'm gonna go. I'm gonna leave. I'm gonna leave. I have sort of a full plate . . . so I'm gonna grab my purse and—"

We could type stuff up really fast because we have the same sense of humor.

ONCE WE'D PERFORMED TOGETHER for a while, Will and I had an agreement that if a sketch was tanking we would just commit harder and harder and never be distracted by the fact that there were no laughs—just give all of our hearts and perform the shit out of it.

We wrote a sketch about a couple who lost a hundred pounds together. It was such a bomb. We did not get a peep of laughter. And we did it center stage. If you do a sketch dead center on the stage, you have a better chance of getting the whole audience with you. But no. Crickets. We didn't care. The more it bombed, the more we kept pushing and committing to it. It was like this *60 Minutes* I saw about a Japanese business school where students who failed would have to crawl into class, to really immerse themselves in failure.

Embracing bombing. Putting success and failure on an equal plane. Seeing the beauty in it.

TO CRACK UP WILL, as well as Jimmy Fallon, who joined the show in 1998, I came up with this character called Jeannie Darcy. It wasn't really for the public; it was more to make my friends laugh. She's a bad stand-up comedian who's always saying, "Don't get me started. Don't even get me started."

The concept was just: she really should not be in show business. She's stiff. She's not a natural performer. But she keeps trying. Working on her act. She has big dreams. She's one of my favorite characters.

I worked on her with Paula Pell and another writer, Scott Wainio. In one sketch that Scott wrote I've got a mullet and I'm doing stand-up comedy in a purple tux with shoulder pads at an old-age home, in front of a fake brick wall that the orderlies roll in behind me. As I do my set, people are actually *dying* and then being *wheeled out*. I don't even notice. I keep doing my stand up.

It's just technical jokes delivered by somebody who should not have gone into comedy. Somebody who's slightly on the spectrum but getting into comedy.

She can't read faces.

She has a hard time telling the difference between a happy face and a sad face.

She's also out of touch with her sexuality and doesn't realize she's gay—so she does straight comedy, talking about her boyfriend. Paula Pell wrote the funniest, corniest, leaving-the-toilet-seat-up-and-other-annoying-stuff-that-men-do jokes.

Jeannie Darcy was also my response as a performer to the need to always be getting laughs.

I thought, *I want to do something that's kind of dull and real. And gets no laughs. And just be okay with this type of quiet, low-key performance.*

Sometimes before the live show people would do *bits* at dinner, and I'd think, *I need a break from comedy just for thirty minutes while I eat. So let's take a break.* Not that people weren't very entertaining. But sometimes I would think, *Do we have to do bits now, at dinner? It's tiring. Don't do your bit. I want to eat and talk seriously.*

I wanted to do something very flat with Jeannie Darcy.

I started doing it for myself as a creative exercise.

But Will and Jimmy would stand by the stage and I could hear them laughing, and so then I mostly did it just for them. To make them laugh.

It wasn't really for the public.

I INITIALLY LIKED COMEDY because I felt like an outsider, so I hate when comedy becomes too cool for school. That's not my thing. Comedy groups that are too cliquey or culty. Comedians are the outsiders, the odd ones, the freaks, the geeks.

I always *wanted* to do a sketch about what my sister Mary and I called Hot Cocoa Girls. Growing up, we were fascinated with girls who'd never really struggled, and when they got a taste of sadness, they would just exaggerate it.

"Oh my God, my *grandpoppy* died"—that would be the hardest thing they'd ever been through in their life. And if they were out at a restaurant, they were usually *chilly* and needed to be *warmed up* by the fire.

"Oh, does anybody have a *shawl* or a *coat*? I'm cold." They were always chilly. "I just need a hot cocoa. I need to be cozy and taken care of. I'm a *baby*. Can someone take care of me?" Girls who could just rest their heads on their sweetie pies' shoulders.

It was an affront to Mary and me what babies some girls got to be. There's a big difference between losing a grandparent as an adult versus losing your parent when you're a kid. It was our reaction to girls who could take for granted having a mommy and a daddy. Girls who didn't struggle much, for whom things came easily, but who *still* want to be rescued from their pain irritated my sister and me. The types of girls who got diamond *"push presents"* from their hubbies, after pushing their babies out, when there was just no struggle.

Until their grandmothers died.

Then they're shivering. They want fuzzy blankets. They need warm beverages and boyfriends. They are needy. Their boyfriends need to remind them to eat. They might even *faint* to get attention. We didn't get to be needy. We had to be tough. So we didn't like girls like that: baby girls.

I was working a one-act-play festival once and there was someone on the production team whom I considered a Hot Cocoa Girl. She was from this wealthy East Coast suburb and things were pretty easy.

I was eating an apple while talking to her. When I finished the apple, I just put the core in my purse. And she was shocked and *so uncomfortable.*

"Oh, you just put *an apple core in your purse?!*"

I thought, *If you think that is strange, if you're freaked out by that, you should know that you don't even have the least idea how much darker things could get.*

MY DAD WAS SO proud of me. Every Sunday morning he would call and we would debrief the show. He would always take notes and try to learn the writers' names.

Talking with my dad about *SNL* reminded me of how he'd

been when I was in elementary and middle school: "Tell me about that girl in your class! Tell me about that kid that you babysat for!" He wanted to hear *everything*.

The fact that I could now share the world of *SNL* with my dad, and that he could enter that world that he always wanted to be in through me, was so deeply satisfying.

Since my dad had always wanted to be an actor but said he didn't have the confidence, when I went and did that for him, it gave him access to a world that he'd always wanted to be a part of. Marci Klein. Lorne Michaels. Jim Downey. Conan O'Brien. Adam Sandler. *I got to give it to him.* It was the greatest that he got to see all that.

He loved it.

And *they* loved him. Everyone at *SNL*. Cast members. Writers. My good friend who ran the talent office, Ayala Cohen. They would always stop by our table at the after-party to say hi. My dad went to Marci Klein's wedding in the Hamptons, and Calvin Klein could not stop talking about how much style my dad had. He kept asking, "Who *is* this dapper gentleman?"

He thought Jim Shannon was this charming, stylish guy.

Creatively, my dad made me feel very free because anything was okay with him. He accepted it all. I remember once when I was in LA I invited a woman I'd befriended at Cravings to come see my stage show. She was my dad's age, an Irish Catholic, a mother with five kids of her own. And she was really nice. But she returned to the restaurant after seeing my show and let me know that she was *disgusted* with Sally O'Malley. And particularly that I hiked up my pants. She told me, "I've never seen anything that's so bawdy." She was very scolding.

I thought, *Ew. I'm glad you're not my mother, because you*

would have really inhibited me and my comedy. My dad just said, "Wonderful!" and gave me an A+. He didn't think anything of it. No shaming.

He watched me pull my pants up as far as they could go and just said, "That's my Molly."

And I realized, all of a sudden, how lucky I was: *Oh God, imagine if I'd had some disapproving, critical mother who expected me to be ladylike?*

My dad had good taste in comedy, comedians, and writing, too.

"That Tracy Morgan, he has natural ability," he said.

There was only one time that he didn't approve of something I did comedy-wise. I was on Martin Short's fake interview show, *Primetime Glick,* and when Martin was in character as Jiminy Glick, this *clueless* talk show host, he asked me about my characters and I said, "A lot of time I'm imitating my dad but I'm doing it as a woman."

"Because your dad is a *cross-dresser!*"

I said, "Noooo."

He said, "But you take characters and you *switch sexes*— you just switch the sex!"

"I guess because my dad's such a dominant figure, I take parts of him and exaggerate them."

"You exaggerate your dad's dominance and then you put a dress on it."

"Maybe."

My dad wasn't happy.

He called me and said, "I did *not* like that Jiminy Glick. He was *so* rude to you."

And I explained, "Daddy, no, that's Martin Short, who you *love,* doing a talk show host *character* he made up!"

DARRELL HAMMOND HAD TAKEN over playing Bill Clinton after Phil Hartman left *SNL*. And when you get asked to do a political figure, it's amazing, because it means you'll be in a lot of stuff and get *written for*.

Then when the Lewinsky scandal broke, Lorne said, "We need a Monica."

And I was cast.

I had to really study. I would listen to tapes of her talking to Linda Tripp and figure out how I was going to do an impression. I really tried to put myself in her shoes.

I never want to make fun of anybody. That has always been important to me. And it was always on my mind when I did the Monica Lewinsky impression. Since we had to do it, I tried to do it as an honest version of a girl who was in love with this guy.

I thought about Brian McCaffrey, this boy I'd had a crush on in high school. More than a crush. I used to *long* for him. I thought he was so cute. I would just stare at him in the hallways, thinking, *Oh, he's adorable.*

Every day would either be a good day or a bad day, depending on whether he looked at me or not.

And if he didn't look back at me, I would be sad. I would draw a sad face in my notebook.

I would go watch Brian play basketball and stare at him. Until one day I passed him in the hallway and he kind of mumbled, "Take a picture, it'll last longer!" And that broke the spell. Oh my God. I was mortified.

So I decided I would perform Monica like an infatuated teenager.

Like *Oh my God, he's, like, so cute.*

She's talking to her girlfriend Linda Tripp, saying, "Can

you believe he's the President? He's the *President*. You gotta listen to this message he just left!"

I understood how she felt. How she was totally enamored with him. And for her their affair was serious and physical. I think she was in love. And maybe he was, too.

But it was so unfair that she went through being portrayed as the girl with the scarlet letter. Obviously it was a terrible time for all involved, but Monica had to take the hardest hit. Thrown under the bus before #MeToo. Both Hillary and Monica got thrown under the bus.

When I met Monica, she was not mad or resentful about the impression. I don't think she minded. I wound up having a tremendous amount of admiration for her and all the work she's done to process through that traumatic time. I think she's great.

THEN DARRELL AND I got invited to the second Clinton inauguration, and I brought my dad. We got flown there on this tiny private plane with all these hard-hitting newspeople. Barbara Walters was one of them, and since my dad had seen her on TV for years and been a big fan, he just said, *"Barbara!"* like he knew her. Like she was his good friend. And she hugged him right back, like she knew him, greeted him back with the same warmth. And he *loved* every second of it.

It was *fancy*. We stayed at this big hotel in Washington. Then—along with Darrell, Cheri, Will and his brother, Pat, and Ryan Shiraki from the talent department, we got invited to this meet-the-press thing with Jane Pauley, Katie Couric, Tom Brokaw, and all these politicians and newspeople. And my dad met Tim Russert.

Tim was so nice, and my dad said, "Oh, Tim, you are *phenomenal*."

We had the time of our lives.

During those *SNL* years he would fly to New York City from Cleveland and get dressed up in his little ascot to come to one of my shows, and he got to meet Marci Klein and Lorne Michaels and see my world. He was in heaven, and people always thought he was charming and adorable.

I remember Will saying, "Oh my God! Your dad is so cute!"

Norm Macdonald said, "He seems like he should be in show business more than you or me."

CHAPTER 17

Superstar and Fritz

N 1998, I WAS DEVELOPING A MARY KATHERINE GALLAGHER movie, *Superstar*. Steve Koren and I would always go on walks together to talk about the plot. At the same time I got cast in the movie *Never Been Kissed*. The lead was Drew Barrymore. And I was amazed how nice she was to the crew, how much she made it a team effort.

Drew and I were trying to think of good directors for *Superstar*. Lorne, who was producing, had suggested Bruce McCulloch from *The Kids in the Hall*. I met with Bruce in LA, and he was just fantastic. I loved him.

But he was heading back to Toronto, where he had a bunch of projects, and told me, "I'm too busy. I just can't do it."

When I told Drew, she immediately said, "What? He said he didn't want to do it?"

"Well, he said it's not the right timing. He can't do it."

I was already thinking about who else could direct.

She just said, "Did you tell him that you would do anything to get him? Did you ask him what his concerns were? What did he say? You need to have a solution and get him back on the phone and call him and beg him. You can't accept that! You have to stop him! Don't let him get on the plane!"

"Really?"

"Yes! Call him!"

She actually sat me down in the room where we were shooting and told me exactly what to say. I took notes. She's an incredibly savvy businesswoman and she knows how to get what she wants and make stuff happen. She coached me.

"Call him and say, 'What can we do to make this work?' Say that you'll do whatever it takes! 'Could you do it this time? This place? With these people? What are your concerns? What do you need? What do you want?' Lay it all out there."

I called Bruce and did exactly what Drew suggested.

I also stared at a candle and prayed.

And he agreed to do it.

Later he told me, "I did the film because of the armpits."

BY THEN GEORGE CHEEKS, who'd gone to Harvard law school, was practicing in New York, so he did my contract for *Superstar*. George really took care of me and also put Brian Smyj in the contract, so I could bring him up to Canada for all my stunts. Steve Koren wrote the script and Will played my love interest, Sky Corrigan.

We were in our thirties, playing Catholic high school students, and I was a little worried about that.

But Lorne said, "It's like *Grease*. Don't overthink it."

I was just getting to know Bruce and wasn't sure if I trusted him. He was trying to do all this "funny Christian stuff." I had to say, "No, no, no, no, no, no. This is *serious*. This is not Monty Python. This girl believes in God, prays to God. This is a very devout Catholic girl whose spiritual life is *big*."

And Bruce really listened to me. He got it. He was an incredible collaborator.

My favorite scene in the movie is the one where I make out with a tree. This was also based on a game my friends Andrew Shaifer and Carrie Aizley and I would play sometimes when we were out having fun.

"Okay," we'd tell each other. "Go say good night to that pole. Tell the pole you had a really good time on the date."

We would do it as a joke to make one another laugh.

We'd always try to do it really believably.

Malcolm Campbell, our great editor, put that scene together in *Superstar*. And it was perfect. We never changed it once. Everyone thought, *Oh, it can't be any better.* It shows how skilled Bruce is. He added a nun watching me kiss the tree. Only a great comedy director would know to do that. And the actress playing the nun just nailed it.

I WENT THROUGH A breakup during the movie and remember being so heartbroken. The night we shot the scene where my character says, "Do you think I'm pretty?" I was so sad, but I used that sadness in the scene. Originally the line was "Do you think I'm ugly?"

But Susan Cavan, our producer, said, "Why don't you ask, 'Do you think I'm pretty?'" And that change, and my genuine sadness, made the scene.

THE ACTUAL FILMING OF SUPERSTAR overlapped with shooting *SNL*. Since I was stressed about balancing it all, Lorne got me a private jet—which was so crazy. I'd be up in Toronto acting in the movie and he would fly writers to me so we could write together at the Four Seasons Hotel. I'd be putting together a sketch while I was shooting and then I'd take the jet back down to New York by myself for the broadcast, just thinking, *This is the fanciest.*

Me, two pilots, and some In-N-Out burgers I'd stopped to get for the flight.

This is bananas, I thought.

I wish somebody could have seen me.

At the end of the movie, Bruce McCulloch had me dive over an orchestra pit. I bounced off of a mini-trampoline and flew ten feet across this opening where the camera was. I started out practicing with Brian just going a foot, then two feet, then three feet. Bruce put the camera in the orchestra pit and Brian stood behind the camera, helping me work up to the point where I was saying, "This is easy! I wanna do it again!" I kept going farther and farther.

WHEN *SUPERSTAR* PREMIERED IN LA, I was so excited. I couldn't believe it. There were billboards everywhere. It was such a big deal for a woman to be in her own movie from *Saturday Night Live.*

I popped on a baseball hat so nobody would recognize me and snuck into a showing at a theater in Burbank. For a while I stood in the back, and I heard all these people whispering at the end of the movie—saying it out loud to themselves: "*Superstar. Superstar.*" I couldn't believe it. Then during another showing I sat next to a boy and his mom. I sneaked a look at him as he was watching the movie (*so sweet*). Then he glanced over at me, back at the screen, then back at me—in shock.

When it was over, he turned to his mom, and said, really seriously, "Mom, I think that's the lady who played the superstar."

I thought, *This is incredible.*

I did this several times, standing in the back of the theaters in a baseball cap. I felt like I was at church. It made me cry. I kneeled down quickly in the back of the theater and said a little prayer: *Thank you, God.* I couldn't believe that I had gotten a movie made and got to be there and watch it. I just thought, *This is unbelievable. I am from Cleveland, Ohio. I didn't know anybody. And I got a movie made.*

I WAS DATING A comedian in New York during the height of *SNL*. I really fell for him but it ended up not being a match. We broke up in 1998 but I had already planned a trip to Boca Raton—paid for the hotel and everything.

So my dad said, "Well, I'll come! It's already *paid for!*"

But when we got to Florida, we had a huge fight. I was trying to set some boundaries and my dad felt threatened. Then he disappeared somewhere in the hotel. He was playing games. Hiding. But I decided not to chase him down.

Let him hide, I thought. *Don't run after him . . . calm yourself down.*

But eventually I got worried and went looking for him. And when I finally found him, sitting in a corner of the lobby, I confronted him. I found myself speaking to him about my mom and the accident, expressing myself in a way I never ever had expressed myself before.

"You talk about yourself—that *you* lost *your* wife," I said. "*We lost our mother!* Do you ever think about *that*? You lost your wife—but Mary and I lost our *mom*. Does that ever *dawn* on you?"

He said, "Molly—Molly. There is not a day that goes by that I don't think about the accident. Not a day goes by when I don't think about that and replay it."

It broke my heart. He'd never said it so openly before. We had never talked about it directly because it was so heavy. But now we had broken through. And it was a very big moment of understanding and forgiveness and compassion.

It. Was. Huge.

"Not a day goes by." *I never knew this.*

When you are living in a house where guilt is alive, it leaves a mark. My dad was coping with guilt as an adult, but we were coping with it as children.

And when you are living in an atmosphere of daily, ever-present guilt, what does that do to children? It changes their souls.

WHEN I STARTED MOVING on by dating and having a career, making my own ties and my own world, it was threatening to my dad. One boyfriend in New York would have to remind me that it was normal to go out and that I didn't have to feel so bad for not including my dad.

"That's normal! You shouldn't have to feel grateful for that. Don't act so grateful!" But I did feel guilty.

When I decided to get serious about romance, I remember having the thought, *God, I'll really have to work at this.*

A friend at *SNL* talked to me a lot about dating. She was this beautiful Jewish girl giving a Catholic girl dating advice.

She said, "Look, it's a business, you know?"

And I thought, *Really?*

"Basically, you have to go on a lot of dates. Go to *everything* you're invited to; if you're invited to a party and you don't want to go, just go. Scout, scout, scout, scout, scout. For twenty minutes. Look and see if there's somebody cute.

Just have half a glass of wine. Don't get yourself dehydrated. When you meet a guy and give him your number, if he calls back fast and knows when to transition from just drinks to a nice dinner, that's a good sign. If he can't show up in a reliable way during the fun part when things are easy, he's out. If he gets slippery within three to five dates, he's out. Those are the avoidant detached types—get out."

So I went on a dating spree. I dated four guys at the same time. And it felt really good to be courted and go out. Some dates were in LA; some were in New York. I would *fly* from New York to LA. Just for a date.

I'm a very serious person. I'm old-fashioned about love. I'm a lot like Mary Katherine Gallagher.

I went out with *venture capitalists*. I was wined and dined. I dated a great guy from Cleveland. I briefly dated a software developer. We went to this wonderful restaurant a couple of times and had this delicious chicken with these diverse, tangy sauces—artichoke garlic aioli, Thai sweet chili—and we talked about whatever while I ate this chicken and dipped the pieces into the otherworldly sauces.

Meanwhile I thought, *God, I think I really like him.*

Then we went back again and had the same chicken and sauces—and I thought, *God, I feel like I'm really falling for him.*

Then we went on a third date to a different restaurant and I suddenly realized—now that the chicken and sauces had been removed—he was kind of boring and it was just the tasty chicken that I loved.

I loooooooooooove chicken.

My friend Lisa Sundstedt told me that this guy had an online dating profile and after I ended things with him he wrote, "And no actresses, please."

IT WAS THROUGH THIS dating spree that I met my husband, Fritz Chesnut.

Jane Pratt, who was the editor of *Sassy* magazine, introduced me to Fritz. She called and said, "I have the perfect guy for you. He's a painter and a surfer."

One night she was out for dinner with him and her then boyfriend and invited me to come along. I liked how he didn't gossip. When we all got up to leave, I noticed his burgundy corduroys and his Chuck Taylors and thought he looked so cute, so I invited him to an upcoming show. I asked one of the *SNL* assistants to call and leave him a message confirming the tickets, but he never called back. Usually when I left tickets for guests they'd call back and I would tell them how to come to the after-party. But since Fritz grabbed the tickets but never called back, I never told him about it. After the show I decided to just go home and had kind of forgotten about him. But then at the last minute I changed my mind and thought, *Oh, maybe I'll just stop by the party for thirty minutes.* Fritz didn't even know about the party, but Jane Pratt had seen him walking home with a friend (a female friend) and swooped them up and brought them. So then I saw him at the party and he was with a girl. I thought, *Oh, maybe that's his girlfriend.* But, as Fritz tells it, the girl was one of his roommates—he lived in a giant loft above a bagel factory in Brooklyn—and he told her to scram so he could spend time with me.

He was so handsome. I paraded him around the *SNL* party, thinking, *I hope people think he's my boyfriend.* We had a blast. Then we said goodbye. He told me he had to go to a wedding in Puerto Rico but would call when he got back in a week. I thought, *We'll see.* But, sure enough, he called me right away when he got back. We went out for sushi. I had told him I liked sushi even though I don't like sushi—and I ate like a bird.

At dinner I said something cynical about love to kind of test him and he shot back, "I believe in love."

Of course, I believed in love, too. I was just kind of feeling him out.

After telling me a few things about his ex, he said matter-of-factly, "Well, on to greener pastures"—which still sticks in my mind. On to greener pastures! Ha!

Then we went to Corner Bistro for drinks and stayed out sooooo late. It was raining and he held me tightly under his umbrella. Someone asked for directions and he spoke Spanish with the guy. I was impressed. I loved how tall he was. I wore platform shoes so I looked tall, too, and could match his height—but he said, "You don't have to do that."

I felt so comfortable with him, I invited him to sleep over—which I actually never do. I liked how he didn't say anything about how small my little studio apartment was. He just said, "Wow, nice view." The next morning, after we woke up, he went out and got me ginger ale. We had another date the following week. I took the subway out to Brooklyn so he could show me his loft—pointing out the walls he'd put up himself to make a room. We sat on his bed to talk and I told him I wanted to take things slowly—backing up from that first night where things had moved a little too quickly. And he seemed disappointed at first. But then he realized I was saying this because I was serious about him and he kicked his legs up in the air on the bed, so excited, and said, "You like me!"

Like: *Hooray!* It was so cute.

And we were off!! Just like that.

HE WOULD ALWAYS ASK me out on another date at the end of our dates. Rock-solid reliable. There were no games. We'd be standing by the subway and he would say, "So I was wondering what you are doing this Thursday night."

About a month or so into dating, I got a little worried and I told him I wanted to talk to him about something.

He came over to my place. I'd lit candles. Turned on Natalie Merchant.

"All right," he said. "What do you want to talk about?"

I had written what I wanted to tell him on notecards and I studied them before I went to go speak to him out in the candlelight.

"I'm interested in getting closer to you and I was wondering if you were interested in continuing to get closer to me," I said.

He looked up and said, "That's all you wanted to talk about?"

"Yeah."

"Well, of course I am!"

I really knew I wanted kids, so we talked about that. I wasn't gonna compromise. If he didn't want kids, I wouldn't have continued dating him. He was younger and wasn't quite ready, so we had to work all that out. Negotiate it. But ultimately he loved how straightforward I was and how I knew what I wanted and was very clear and direct.

"*Well*, some guys would run for the hills," he said.

"Well, then you should run for the hills. But just know that I'm not going to compromise that."

I didn't want to hurt his feelings, but I was thirty-six and I didn't have years to mess around. If he had said on the fifth date, "I don't ever want kids," I wouldn't have kept dating him. But Fritz loved how direct I was. He hated flaky girls and appreciated my seriousness about romance.

Before I met Fritz I longed for guys who were unavailable.

Who couldn't quite do it. Who weren't really ready. I grieved my mom through men. It's easy to blame the guy—*What an asshole,* etc. But I always felt less victimized if I asked myself, *What is your part, Molly? What does it say about you that you picked him?* And what it says about me is that, before Fritz, I picked men who couldn't really do it because I was scared shitless myself. *I* wasn't really ready, either. It wasn't just the guys' fault. I was scared of intimacy, too. It meant I might get swallowed up if it was someone who was ready to go. I picked men who were less available for a reason. And when I was ready and more available myself, I chose Fritz.

PART FOUR

GOOD ENDINGS

CHAPTER 18

Leaving *SNL*

ABOUT A YEAR AFTER I MET FRITZ, I GOT NOMINATED for an Emmy for *Saturday Night Live*—a huge deal for me. I remember doing a handstand in my little studio apartment because I was so excited.

I shouted, "Yippee!" all by myself.

A woman from *SNL* hadn't been nominated in over twenty years. Not since Jane Curtin in 1978. This was before there was a separate Variety Show category, so I was up against Cher, Billy Crystal, Chris Rock, and Eddie Izzard in the Outstanding Performance in a Variety or Music Program category. I was thrilled.

I DECIDED TO LEAVE *SNL* after the 2000–2001 season. I wasn't leaving to do a TV show or a movie. I was just leaving because I wanted to develop a personal life. I had been so work oriented for so long. Some people leave and they want to just *work, work, work* more—and I was *not* like that. I wanted to get coffee with friends and start a family. I wanted to enjoy my life and take a break from work. And I wanted to spend more time with my dad. So I wasn't leaving to *go* anywhere. I just felt that it was time.

I wanted a good ending. I only knew awful, abrupt endings because of my childhood. Because I treasured and loved my time at *SNL,* I really yearned for a good ending. I was particularly worried about how Lorne would feel. I was so grateful for the opportunity he'd given me and the kindness with which he had treated me throughout my time on the show. I talked with him a lot in the months leading up to my decision. It was very hard to go, because it's such a special place. But because I had done it for six full seasons, because I loved it so much, I really wanted to leave when I *still* loved it and I wanted to leave with dignity and thoughtfulness because I cared so much about Lorne and the show. I didn't want to stay on too long, phoning it in. I wanted to leave in the most respectful, loving way.

I also thought, *You've got to pass the torch to other young, hungry performers ready for that opportunity.*

I said all that to Lorne and he was really understanding about my decision. He didn't want me to leave, but he honored my hopes to take it all slowly and make the most of my last few months on *SNL.*

The perceptive Tina Fey, who'd just started doing "Weekend Update," told me, "Lorne is not really accepting the fact that you are leaving."

But as Lorne and I kept talking, we came up with a plan. I would leave the show in February and come back for a prime-time special that was scheduled for Mother's Day.

I said, "I really wanna come back and do it."

And Lorne said, "Of course."

All the cast mothers would be performing with their kids.

And my mom for the night would be my dad. I would've stayed and finished out the season if I couldn't have come back for this show. That's how important it was for me that my dad got to be on the show.

Maya Rudolph, whose mother, the singer Minnie Riperton, had died when Maya was six, was going to have her dad there, too.

After we came up with that plan, a going-away announcement came out in the *New York Times*.

My dad said he liked how sad I looked in the photo accompanying the announcement.

"It shows how much you care, Molly."

IN FEBRUARY MY DAD flew out to see me in my last-ever *SNL*. I'd also invited Fritz and his dad to be there. Before coming downtown to my place, my dad stopped at the Hyatt Regency bar near Grand Central, where he met a straight, preppy, super-nice college boy and brought him back to my place downtown. And so here's this college-age stranger in my apartment (I'd moved to a bigger one-bedroom) with my dad. It was the first time in a very long time I had seen my dad drunk. He had been sober for years.

He started slurring, "Mollllly, this, this is David. He's a college student."

And I was so mad at him. This was a big week for me. It was Thursday. I was on the way out the door to rehearse for my very last show.

But I decided that we should eat something—or he should, to sober up. So we all went out to the Tavern on Jane for burgers. The kid just sat there while my dad and I had a fight. I was so mad and so mean. And I thought, *Oh, this poor kid in the middle of all this darkness.*

To this day, I do not know who this kid was or what my dad had told him. I felt very sorry for him for having to see all of that. He was really nice.

He was drinking, too. Maybe that made it less awkward for him. Anyway, at some point he left.

And I ended up telling my dad he couldn't stay with me— that he had to go stay in a hotel. I wasn't being codependent. I'd never really done anything like that to him before.

I remember thinking the whole scene was pathetic and sad. But I was so mad at him for drinking and making it all about him.

AFTER I MADE MY DAD stay at the hotel, I called Steven Levy and told him about the whole flare-up.

"I'm so pissed off at my dad. He showed up drinking. He brought this poor kid along."

But Steven kept defending him. It was weird. Instead of sympathizing with me, he said, "Molly, you are being too hard on him. You don't understand how much he's given up for you and Mary. He's sacrificed so much of himself, so much of his life, for you."

I couldn't believe what I was hearing. Eventually I cut him off and said, "What are you talking about? Why are you defending him like that? What are you trying to say?"

Then something clicked in my head. Steven is gay. I paused for a second and asked, "Are you saying he's gay?"

"I don't want to say anything! He wants to tell you. But he's scared. He's going to tell you."

Wow. Oh my God. Oh my God.

"We've been talking," Steven continued, "and he's ready for you to know. He just doesn't know how to tell you."

He's going to tell me!

In that moment, and all at once, I felt my heart grow a thousand sizes. All the pieces began to fit together. I was so excited and started making plans for him. He was going to go dancing at gay clubs. He was going to fall in love. My head went wild with visions of his new life as an openly gay man.

He was going to be just like Christopher Plummer in *Beginners*!

Suddenly everything made sense—the craziness, the drinking, the anger. I realized he hadn't gotten to be himself. Deep compassion, love, and understanding just flooded in.

I told Fritz, but Fritz was cautious.

"I don't know," he said. "He's pretty old."

I wish I had known this about my dad before, I thought. *I could have talked to him.*

The next morning I walked over to his hotel and found him on the street outside, getting cash at an ATM and shivering so hard. He said, "I'm gonna just go home." He said there hadn't been any heat in his room. He was cold all night long. But he started to calm down after a few minutes. We called a truce and went to my favorite little coffee shop, La Bonbonniere, across the street from his hotel, where a very warm and kind waitress named Marina went out of her way to make us both feel better. (She knew my dad from all the trips he made to visit me in New York City when I was doing *SNL*.)

After we got a table and I said, "Look, this last show is a big deal for me and I was just disappointed that you showed up drinking. It makes me feel stressed."

He understood and really apologized.

So he decided not to leave.

And I let him come back up and stay at my apartment.

(Yay!)

MY DAD HAD OPENED UP to Steven Levy about a year before. Steven had called him on the phone after having dinner with us one night and just spoken his mind.

"Jim: You're gay!"

My dad said, "Yes, I probably am."

They started exchanging stories and talking through all the challenges they had both faced.

Steven had lost his father as a young boy, so I think he saw the relationship with my dad as a chance to help someone, to be a good surrogate son. And once they got to know each other, he talked on the phone a lot with my dad. It was thanks to my dad's advice that Steven met his now husband, Bill Neil. ("Steven, if you don't have a good time at a party, it's your own damn fault. You need to go over and introduce yourself to the person who doesn't have anyone to talk to. You need to extend yourself and go ask them questions.")

He would also send my dad gay porn, wrapped and taped up in shopping bags in case someone else acccidentally opened it.

"Oh my God, Steven, their cocks are huge!" my dad said.

I didn't really know if my dad was gay or bi. He dated one woman seriously for many years but I knew he wasn't in love with her. Then he dated a sexy young college professor who he was crazy about. He said she really knew how to make a man feel like a man. I would wonder about his sexuality sometimes and then I would push away the thought. When Fritz met my dad, he said, "You know your dad has a real queenie side."

I just said, "What? A *queenie* side? What do you mean?!"

But now pieces from the past began to fit together. There had certainly been signs. But I never fully acknowledged that he might be gay. I used to buy little headshots of Joan Crawford or Bette Davis, sign them, and add a little message— "Dear Daddy, NYU is great. Look at Joan."

But it did not dawn on me that he was gay or bi. I just thought, *Daddy will love this.*

Like when I saved up all my money to get new, expensive, full-color headshots and after I mailed him one he got out the glue, threw sparkles all around my face, and framed it.

Or when my dad and Mary and I watched this movie on TV, *Ode to Billy Joe,* starring Robby Benson and Glynnis O'Connor. It was about a closeted country boy in Mississippi who has sex with a man and commits suicide by jumping off the Tallahatchie Bridge, and was based on the country song "Ode to Billie Joe" by Bobbie Gentry. (Mary and I didn't understand the ending, but I remember my dad getting emotional. Now it seems impossible that they even *put* a movie like that on television in the 1970s. And, of course, much later I would reference the kinds of movies that I grew up on in MKG's dramatic monologues.)

The way my dad would be so enamored with some of my male friends and say, "Wow! He is *movie star handsome!*"

He *loved* Jimmy Fallon and he would say, "You should be with someone like Jimmy."

I would say, "Oh—Jimmy is my friend," and think, *It seems more like* he *wants to be with Jimmy.*

But I never saw any of that as part of his sexuality.

JUST A FEW MONTHS before I learned that my dad was gay (or bi—I always say "or bi," since he didn't live to describe his sexuality, and I want to be respectful. . . . so maybe queer, or no label), he'd been trying to give up smoking. His method was to smoke cigarettes slowly, glamorously, while looking in the mirror very intently. He'd heard that if you watched your-self smoking and really meditated on what you were trying to stop doing, it would help you quit. But it was so dramatic and so glam. My brother-in-law saw him doing it and thought it was hilarious.

"Your dad is *so* eccentric," he told Mary.

THE NIGHT AFTER THE fight and my finding out about my dad's sexuality, Lorne and Marci threw me a big farewell party at the Hudson Hotel, and I saw my dad and the world through new eyes. This giant thing had been revealed to me, and I'd told Fritz, who was very excited and happy for me. But I didn't say anything to my dad.

He was wearing this camel overcoat over a tailored black suit, and he looked so elegant. It was the opposite of the previ-ous night. My dad was amazing. Stone sober of course. I felt such deep love for my dad that night. He talked to everyone and made real connections. The party was so much fun. Brian Smyj presented me with all my padding as a going-away gift. Toasts were made. It was a magical night. I honestly felt that I could retire right there.

My dad talked to both Marci and Lorne for a long time and really connected with them.

I remember feeling incredible understanding for my dad, now that I knew this truth about his sexuality.

Right as I was having these thoughts, Marci came up to

me, tears in her eyes, and told me, "James Shannon! I love that man! You don't understand. I love your dad." She also told me she wanted to marry my dad.

MY DAD WROTE THIS letter of thanks to Lorne:

To my friend

Mr. Lorne Michaels

Thank you for giving Molly the break of her life on Saturday Night Live, and also the many kindnesses you have given her and numerous others in launching their careers. You are a very special person and your kindness knows no bounds.

Your special interest in her career is deeply appreciated by me, also thanks for the wonderful party you gave at the Hudson Hotel Penthouse, and also for inviting me to be a part of the Mother's day special. Words can not express the many thoughtful things you have done.

Sincerely,
Jim Shannon

CHAPTER 19

My Mom

SHORTLY AFTER THE TRIP TO BOCA RATON I GOT A LETTER with a Cleveland postmark. My dad had asked my mom's good childhood friend Jeanne McConville to get in touch with me:

Dear Molly . . .

Your mom was my friend. She lived down the street from me on West 101st St. We walked together every day to St. Ignatius grammar school from the 4th thru 8th grade.

Mrs. Keating (your grandmother) made hot oatmeal every morning before leaving for work. Your mom and her brother Hubert would put the oatmeal into two bowls, throw out the cereal, + then put the two dirty cereal bowls in the sink, so it looked like they ate the cereal. I really don't know if Hughie ever ate the "mush" or not, but I know Peggy ate saltine crackers + a bottle of Pepsi for breakfast every morning. . . .

Mrs. Keating your grandmother was a very kind + generous lady who spoke English with a thick Irish brogue. They often had relatives from Ireland staying at their house for long periods.

Mrs. Keating supported the family with the salary she earned working in a factory.

Mr. Keating adored his beautiful Peggy, but he had a drinking problem and was unable to keep a job. Peggy lived in fear of someone coming over to her house and seeing her father on one of his bad days. This was very stressful for her. She loved her dad.

MY MATERNAL GRANDPARENTS CAME over from County Mayo, on the wild west coast of Ireland. My grandfather, Owen Cattigan, who changed his name to Keating when he came to America, was from Achill Island, and my grandmother, Mary Madden, was from Corraun. The two places are only a couple hundred feet apart—separated by the Achill Sound—but my grandparents never knew each other in Ireland. They met in the US, married, and had my uncle Hugh and my mom.

The Keatings lived on the west side of Cleveland, which was full of Irish immigrants. Everyone liked Mary Madden, my grandmother. She was a happy woman. On Thursdays her friends would come over and they'd drink whiskey together. They'd be drinking and smoking.

My grandfather fell into dark moods and went in and out of jobs. My grandmother liked to say, "He's a good man as long as he isn't drinking." But because he couldn't stop drinking, she was really the one who had to work, so she became a maid.

My mom and my uncle Hugh were latchkey kids. They had it tough. But they also had each other.

Sometimes they'd come home from school and find their

dad passed out on the front lawn. Uncle Hugh told me that when he skipped school once, this nun, Sister Gil, tracked down my mom and told her, "Peggy, go home and tell your mother what Hugh did."

But instead she stood on the corner waiting to warn him.

Uncle Hugh said, "Don't tell Mom!" and she didn't.

They really looked out for each other. They were *close*.

AS ADULTS, MY MOM and my uncle wrote long letters to each other. In one he asked her, "What are you going to do after you graduate high school . . . go to college or are you going to work?"

Because she loved books and wanted to teach reading and work as a librarian, she went to college and studied library science. But while she was in school, her mom died very suddenly. At the funeral her mother's friends all told her, "Oh, she was so proud of you." She'd never known.

After college my mom got a job as a librarian at Woodland Hills Elementary School, on the east side of Cleveland, way across town from where she'd grown up. My mom was passionate about getting kids to read.

When my parents met, my dad didn't say much about my mom to his family.

Usually, according to one of his sisters, my aunt Mary Rita, when he dated a girl, he'd immediately start picking her apart.

But all he said about my mom was "She's really smart."

And my aunt knew, *This is it. This is the girl*.

Uncle Hugh thought my dad was "a Fancy Dan—a well-dressed guy from Shaker Heights."

He told me my mom was so excited. "She was a West Side

girl, an Irish immigrant, and just head over heels. Peggy wasn't normally like that."

June Rini, my mom's best buddy from high school, told me, "I'll never forget when she met your dad—she described him as Clark Gable, Jack Kennedy, and Robert Redford—all rolled into one! He was the handsomest guy and she was in love!"

My mom wrote my dad a lot of letters:

Tuesday

Hello, you old bachelor,

I hope you're not having too good a time. I feel very disappointed tonight because as yet I haven't heard from you. Earlier this evening the phone rang while I was taking a bath. Thinking it might be you I jumped out of the tub dripping wet to answer it. It was one of my father's friends. . . .

We had a very pleasant day at work today—laughed all day.

It is already 10:30 and I haven't really accomplished too much at home tonight—very discouraging.

I don't really feel like writing too much more. Maybe tomorrow at work I'll dash off a line. My main purpose in writing was just to remind you that I love you and need you very much.

Do you think of me very often? You are on my mind every minute of the day. I say to myself, "I wonder what my 'wootsie's' doing." Then I think, oh, he's probably so homesick for me. Then again I think—I don't know—

*maybe, he's not even thinking about me. For a moment
I'll get very generous and think—well just as long as he's
happy—that's all that counts. Then again, in my more
selfish moments I'll say to myself, "I hope he's not having
too good a time. What it all boils down to is that I really
want the best of happiness and good luck for you but in
the process I don't want you to love me less or take me for
granted. I don't think I could ever take you for granted.*

Well, anyhow, good night, I've been talking in circles.
Instead, I'll be square *with you and tell you how much I
deeply love you. . . . Goodnight, nice boy.*

> *All my love,*
> *Peggy*

AFTER I WAS BORN, my mom called her father and he didn't
pick up. My dad drove her over to his place on Olympia Road.
She carried me inside to check on him while my dad waited in
the car with my sister Mary.

My dad waited such a long time that he started to wonder, *What is taking Peg so long?* He went in and found her in
shock, holding me beside her father, who was passed out on
the table, dead.

My dad always said because my mom had been used to
dealing with drinkers, she knew how to subtly get the point
across that she was disappointed. She didn't raise her voice.
She would just leave his dinner out and remove herself without a word.

My mom's dad was an alcoholic and then she married an
alcoholic, the vicious generational cycles of alcoholism.

WHEN I WAS READY to really deal with my mom's death, when I was in my thirties I sought out my uncle Hugh. He was a tall, smart, stoic, handsome Irish guy who, like a lot of Irish immigrants, didn't have a formal education. But he built a very big successful plumbing business and made good investments in real estate.

I wanted to hear about my mom from her brother's perspective, and he was so happy I was reaching out.

"Your mom was the best," he said. "Believe me. I loved her. She was tough in defending me when we were kids. But later she had a problem with my drinking. She felt I shouldn't do it. And then your *father* defended me."

I asked Uncle Hugh how he coped with my mom's death.

"Boy, in hell. I'm starting to cry right now. I was in such shock. I took over a year to get over it. I went back to the scene of the accident and really studied it to figure out what had happened. The pole he hit was bent in two different places. After your accident, they no longer permitted this type of light pole. They started to put them on a concrete foundation with an aluminum base. It was right before the ramp on Superior, in St. Clare. 1968. Over forty years ago. . . . And then I spent all this time at the funeral home.

"There were arguments about where your mom would be laid out after the accident. I wanted the funeral on the West Side but it ended up on the East Side, at the Schulte Funeral Home. After that I really just disappeared. I took off after she died. I was never the same. I went on a drinking bender."

On the phone he told me, "My father was a drunk. I was a drunk. But it wasn't hard for me to quit drinking. I eventually really hustled and got sober in AA. My sponsor told me, 'Don't worry about the steps and all that BS—just don't drink.'"

And once Hugh stopped drinking, he was unstoppable. He was elected the first business manager of the Cleveland Plumbers Union, Local 55, when they were building huge projects, like the Perry Nuclear Power Plant on Lake Erie.

"Were you angry at my dad after the accident?" I asked.

"I never got angry. I got distant from him. And I stayed distant. I figured he fell asleep at the wheel. It's a long drive. You get tired. After that, your dad would call sometimes when he was drinking, and he confided in me that he never got over the guilt of the accident. He couldn't get over it. He didn't want to live."

RECENTLY, AS I WAS finishing this book, John Goulet, the counterman at Sand's Deli, where we used to go after church, told me he remembered hearing about our car accident. His sister came up screaming to him how Peg Shannon, Katie, and Fran had been killed.

She'd told him, "They were killed on Dead Man's Curve in an automobile accident."

John explained, "On the shoreway when it turns into the inner belt past East Ninth Street, left two lanes—that's Dead Man's Curve. When trucks hit that in the past, they would overturn. Lots of accidents."

Dead Man's Curve. I never knew it was called that.

AFTER I SPOKE WITH Uncle Hugh, my sister Mary sent me a list called "Things I Remember About Mommy." I was so little when she died, I didn't remember any of what Mary remembered. It was so thoughtful of her to send me this.

- she liked pepsi, butter mints & onions

- she liked the "dancing bear" from Captain Kangaroo (we would get her when he came on)

- she liked to stop at the "frosty" counter at Higbee's (downtown), I think she knew the people who worked there

- she used to sing & dance with us (dance with a dolly with a hole in her stocking)

- she read us lots of Dr. Seuss books, Little Bear and Little Black Sambo

- when I was in first grade she helped me with my homework every night and tried to make a game out of learning by letting me take a step around the dining table every time I got a flash card right (she made the flash cards)

- in the middle of the night she would allow us to come down and bring cereal boxes (Quisp & Captain Crunch) up to our beds

- she would give us butter & saltine crackers & peanut butter crackers

- you Mommy and Katie would pick up me and some friends from school, she would bring Ritz crackers & kool-aid in Dixie cups for all of us (we had a picnic) before going to after school activities

- she taught me how to walk to St. Dominics

- she took piano lessons

- she encouraged us to draw

I remember our mom chasing me and my two sisters up the steps, grabbing our toes, saying, "I'm gonna get your little piggies!" I don't have many memories of her but this is a strong one. A joyful, playful one.

AT THE FUNERAL, ONE side of the church was so full of mourners, it seemed like the whole West Side had come. And that entire side of the church was just crying. Uncle Hugh told me, "Your mom had so many friends. People loved her. She was so kind. It was a mistake that she and your father moved to Shaker Heights. Her friends were all from the West Side. The East Siders were more aggressive and your mom wasn't used to that. She was used to West Side girls. West Side people."

My grandmother's brother was a priest, Father Willie Madden, who also came over to Cleveland from Corraun.

Mary told me: "Father Willy said . . . he has *NEVER* been to a sadder funeral than Mommy's, Katies & Fran. He said . . . all the caskets in the aisle. . . . I forget who else told me . . . the wailing from the West Side of Cleveland was immense."

AFTER MY MOM DIED the kids she taught wrote down their memories of her. I have all these sweet notes from her students:

"Whenever we think about books full of good stories we'll remember our friend."

"I am writing a poem about Mrs. Shannon."

"She told us so many good stories."

"She liked to smile and laugh."

"I remember the fun work Mrs. Shannon gave us."

"She was the best library teacher we ever had."

"Big book, small book, Mrs. Shannon was chief of all books."

"I remember Mrs. Shannon when she helped me find a book about electronic brains and iron and steel."

"I remember she was always smiling."

"I remember the time Mrs. Shannon took us outside, and we sat in the grass, and read The Book of Riddles."

"She was lovable, truthful, honorable, and best of all she was my friend."

While working on this memoir, I found some pages my dad had written about my mom after the accident. He wrote,

> After we got in bed at the end of a full day Peg would light up a cigarette, often her first of the day and she loved to talk about what Mary or Molly or Katie did or said what they had learned. Their new expressions of anger, happiness, fear or how cute this was or how funny that mad expression on Katie's face was when she didn't want to do what she was told. I could tell

from Peg's voice how much she thoroughly enjoyed talking about her children. It is indeed a great consolation to me now remembering the many times we impulsively decided to take the girls to go out to a nice restaurant and have an enjoyable time as a family. Or stop at a summer carnival on our way to visit someone or have a picnic on the spur of a moment at a pleasant little park not far from our home just to see the kids have fun or a Sunday at the zoo or hamburgers on the way home. Christmas, Santa Claus, the bunny, Halloween, the wicked witches and pumpkins, those colorful drives in autumn. Thanksgiving and the feast of turkey with friends. These are the memories I will long cherish of our life together. Or the time she was completely surprised with the diamond ring I gave her for Christmas which matched her engagement ring at a time when we certainly couldn't afford it but somehow always managed to pay for and the many other things we did and couldn't afford. These are the days I'll always remember and I pray Mary and Molly will remember their mother and all the happy times when they look at all those snapshots. What never ceased to amaze me was her talent to make friends with such a variety of people, the compassion and understanding she had for the poor, underprivileged, the uneducated and the overindulgent rich but mostly for her fellow man in general. My wife's persistence in learning to play the piano at an age when most women are thinking of less taxing recreations and the pride she enjoyed in her accomplishment seeing the pleasure it gave us listening to her play her latest song or my favorite Laura's theme with the children playing before a crackling fire while I lay on the couch. To have the room completed before the children made a mess of everything. Before we could clean it up, the happiness in seeing our labors make for a more beautiful home with the main ingredient love apparent in our communication with one another. Weekend vacations with other couples to nearby towns or the real big city ski resort where her persistence to manage the slopes was impressive, her inquisitiveness and sailing on our first date and her enthusiasm wanting to buy a boat enumerating what family fun it would be or the time we decided to buy a camper and just take off for a month and visit places we had never been before and new spots for summer.

Thank God I have these memories. Her love of life or the time we took horseback riding lessons, her fear a little obvious and her desire to be an observer on our first visit to the riding academy but she wasn't an observer long—it was after several lessons that she finally decided that she didn't think it necessary to follow all the protocol of English riding as she had no intention of ever entering any shows. The fact that it was so expensive and she could never keep up with the horsey set. But nothing ventured, nothing gained was her motto as we continued to pursue new activities even if some of them didn't last very long. I'll never forget the stimulating effect Peg had on me when the new brochures arrived in fall and winter offering a variety of courses for adults in Shaker school system and her enrolling in tennis one semester Spanish another time speed reading another time and the exhausting research she just finished in basic reference for additional credit to aid her in library science. The regrettable fact is that after all her exhausting work she never lived to learn that she received an A in the course but I'm sure she has better than an A plus now.

In one of her many letters to my dad, my mother wrote, "My morning at work was very lonely without your phone call. I had nothing to look forward to. I love you very much and if I permitted myself I would miss you frantically. However, I am not permitting myself so I just miss you very, very, very much. Yes such a nice boy. Be very careful driving home. Don't drive if you're tired and don't drink when you're driving."

CHAPTER 20

Coming Out

WE WROTE AND REHEARSED THE MOTHER'S DAY SPE-
cial during the first week of May 2001. Then it
was pre-taped and broadcast on Sunday the thir-
teenth. All the mothers (and the two dads) did a song in the
opening monologue. And each parent got to do a sketch with
their son or daughter.

"Daddy," I said as we rehearsed, "you are singing off key."
I remember Chris Kattan turned around and started laughing when I said that. "You are throwing everyone off. Just
mouth the words."

And then the choreography was confusing, too.

Paula Pell told me, "Oh, don't worry. It's fine if your dad
wants to make up his own steps. He's doing his own thing—
his own dance."

He had been so encouraging to me so this was a small gift
I could give him back. And it was so much fun having my
dad with me as we went to Hair and Makeup and rehearsed in
front of an audience together. When he bumped into Renée
Zellweger after the live show (she was the host), she gave
him *so many* kisses on the cheek. He said she reminded him

of Judy Garland—and this was way before she played Judy Garland!

DURING THE MOTHER'S DAY rehearsals, I came into the dressing room and found my dad shivering and closing his eyes for quick little naps, tired. He was with all the moms, waiting to rehearse. Will Ferrell's mom, Kay, put her hand on my dad's shoulder and said, "*Jim.* Jim, I'm worried about you. *Jim.* Put a sweater on."

He seemed weak, frail, off—and I got a little frustrated that he couldn't pull it together for our father-daughter pre-taped bit.

He just said, "This is exhausting. There's a hell of a lot people don't realize about how much goes into it."

AFTER REHEARSAL ONE EVENING, we walked back to the Palace Hotel on Madison and Fiftieth. Ayala, my friend who worked in the talent department at *SNL*, had arranged for him to stay there because he'd told her, "I want to be close to St. Patrick's Cathedral."

Though when Ayala asked if he wanted a massage or pedicure, he told her no.

"More for ladies," he said.

Now we were just sitting in his room, talking. He looked like he was going to confide in me, and I thought, *He's going to tell me!*

Ever since my conversation with Steven Levy in February, Steven had been saying about my dad, "He's going to tell you. He's going to tell you." So that's what I was expecting.

Instead he said, "Molly, I have prostate cancer."

And I started crying so hard. All his behavior over the last few months made sense now: the shivering, the tiredness, the weight loss, the drinking when he came for my last *SNL*. He had cancer. He was scared. He had been jealous that I'd also invited Fritz's dad to my last show. Keeping so much bottled up inside, it was no wonder he wanted to drink. For months he had chosen to keep his cancer private, but now he was telling me.

He also told me he had tape-recorded a conversation with Dr. Martin Resnick, the director of urology at University Hospitals of Cleveland, discussing the hormone therapy drug, Lupron, which Dr. Resnick recommended for my dad. My dad asked if he could play it back for me.

Sitting there together, I heard my dad tell Dr. Resnick, "I do have a death wish."

AT THE TIME GEORGE Cheeks was dating a doctor, Larry Hausman, who treated cancer patients at Mount Sinai Hospital in New York. When I told George about my dad's cancer, he put his boyfriend in touch with me.

Larry gave me some facts about my dad's hormone treatment, which would reduce his testosterone, saying, "Lupron will keep him alive longer and the side effects aren't bad. But the best thing you can do is be around him."

My dad joked that, since he was getting female hormone shots, he was going to buy a dress.

AFTER THE MOTHER'S DAY special aired, a beautiful piece about my dad came out in the *Cleveland Plain Dealer*.

The article was written by their TV critic, Tom Feran,

and illustrated with a big picture of my dad and me during the special.

I called my dad to celebrate but he seemed disappointed.

"Oh, Molly," he said. "I looked so *thin* on TV. I hated the way that I looked. I looked just terrible."

It stabbed me in the heart. I had made his dream come true, and he couldn't fully enjoy it. I finally got him on TV but he was *sick*. I tried to cheer him up: "Daddy, all actors think they look terrible on TV. I can't stand seeing myself on screen. *Most* people think that. Welcome to showbiz! We are all hard on ourselves."

"Is that right? Oh, that makes me feel so much better," he said.

I said, "A lot of people don't even watch themselves, ever. I thought you looked good!"

Then he read the article out loud to me on the phone, and he started crying. He loved it.

Lorne always said he could be in the *New York Times* and his mom wouldn't be impressed—but when there was an article about him in *her* local paper, it was such a big, big deal. And it meant so much to my dad to be in his hometown paper.

SHORTLY AFTER THAT, in June of 2001, Fritz and I went on an all-expenses-paid safari in Zimbabwe for a travel show. My dad seemed to be doing well with his cancer treatments, and Fritz and I wanted a chance to spend some time traveling together.

We were out looking at lions every day from these open-air vehicles. Our guide kept pointing out the *old* lions.

When the older male lions know that they are dying, they

go off by themselves. I remember feeling so sad about those old lions. I felt sad that they needed to be private when they were failing. That they started separating from their loved ones. That they were so tired.

The end of life.

I was thinking a lot about lions dying.

These lions!

And my dad was really on my mind.

My dad kept calling me on the trip. We had these long conversations in Africa when I could tell he really needed me. He was pulling toward me and asking me about everything in my life. He was the opposite of the lions. He was trying to come close, not pull away. And I felt close to him. I think it was hard for him because I was so far away.

But in my gut I was worried.

Even though coming closer was the opposite of how the lions died, I still kept thinking of my dad and these elderly male lions in the same way.

Maybe he's like the lions. Maybe he's dying, too.

AFTER RETURNING FROM SAFARI, I went on a press junket for the film *Serendipity*. I played the best friend of the main character, Kate Beckinsale.

At one point in the movie, there's this mix-up where somebody's parents think her character and my character are a couple.

My favorite moment filming was when I asked the director, Peter Chelsom, "Can I say, when I see off Kate, 'Goodbye, my sweet lesbian lady lover'?"

He hesitated. Once again it didn't look like a joke on paper. But he couldn't tell how I was going to say it, hitting all the *L*'s *really hard*—"Goodbye, my sweet *L*esbian *L*ady *L*over!"

I loved the way it sounded. It was that comedy-as-music idea. And when he let me try it, it got a huge laugh.

KNOWING THAT MY DAD was sick, I invited him to fly out to LA on August twenty-second and join me for the *Serendipity* junket. The studio was putting us up at the Four Seasons and I thought it would be so fun for my dad and me.

We went to the premiere together and afterward I felt this urgency for him to see all my friends. So I planned dinners. I thought it would be fun for him. One night a dinner with Will Ferrell, his wife, Viveca Paulin-Ferrell, and Heather Graham at Asia de Cuba . . . and then another dinner with my friend Mike Rad at Locanda Veneta . . . and a dinner with Eugene Pack, his wife, Dayle Reyfel, and Alison Earle (who'd moved to Santa Barbara) and her husband, Jim, at Pane e Vino . . . and then another dinner with Steven Levy and his mom at Spago . . . my friend John Hoffman and his boyfriend Tony Leondis at Orso.

Every. Single. Night. Out. With. Friends.

My dad thought it was so sweet, but he felt bad he didn't have his usual energy.

He said, "I really just want to hang out with you."

We also went to see my amazing therapist. He got all dressed up for the session, in a white turtleneck and a white sweater with a shamrock stitched on it. When she told him he'd had to play both parental roles, mother and father, he liked that a lot.

"I never thought of it that way," he said.

MY DAD WAS SO friendly to everyone at the Four Seasons. They all knew him and liked him, and for years afterward, whenever I went back to the hotel, they all asked about my dad.

We called Dr. Resnick in Cleveland to get the results of my dad's recent PSA test and were so relieved because the numbers looked okay.

Then we paged Dr. Larry Hausman, George Cheeks's boyfriend, and when he heard the numbers he said, "He's doing well."

It was good news! My dad was very happy.

"Oh, good—good. You don't know how relieved and happy that makes me feel!" he said.

We had adjoining rooms at the Four Seasons, and it was *sooooooo* fancy and fun. Since he still had not told me about being gay—or bi—I thought, *I'm just going to ask him.*

We went out to the pool. It was a gorgeous, sunny day and we were sitting on the lounge chairs next to the water, eating Cobb salads in our cozy white hotel robes.

I took a deep breath and seized the chance to ask *the million-dollar question* that a child can only ask a parent when they are still alive.

"Have you ever thought you might be gay?"

Eight words.

When I said it, I saw a plane pulling a banner with my words on it across my eyes, with a huge question mark at the end.

Here we go. This is the question that has always needed to be asked but has never been asked. Here we are—the million-dollar moment!!

He instantly responded, "*Most* definitely."

Really? Wow! Wait, what did he just say? Heart beating fast. *I can't believe what I am hearing. Holy shit! Ohmygodohmygodohmygod.*

We moved over to another part of the pool. Since he seemed so open and willing to talk, I asked more questions.

The conversation continued for the next seventy-two hours. After the press junket was over, we drove up to Ojai, about ninety minutes north of LA, and continued talking about everything.

We stopped at the Carrows diner when we got there and sat for hours and hours as he told me about this hidden part of his life. He had a fruit cup and I had an Irish cream coffee. It was fantastic. I got to ask him anything and everything.

"Oh, Molly, I knew when I was in eighth grade. I would go on double dates with girls, but I always liked the *boy*. I had a crush on this Polish boy. I liked the way his fingers held his cigarette—his hand looked glamorous. I would try to hold my cigarette like him. I liked how he looked so macho. I also used to look at men in their undershirts in magazines. I liked their big builds. I wished I could be built like that.

"I tried to tell your mom. Right around the time you were born, I even went to a psychiatrist who told me I was a 'latent homosexual.' I told your mom when I got home from the appointment, straight out. She got mad. She didn't want to hear it. She told me the therapist should never have said that to me."

When he went to conventions and on business trips, sometimes men would give him the eye and slip their business cards into his pocket. He said it made him feel all mixed up. *I don't want to take your card. But I do. But I don't. But I do! How dare you?!* He felt mad at the men—mad but intrigued. He told me his gay life was mostly limited to occasional blow jobs at bars and truck stops, a common practice in that day and age and something that he and many others did due to the closeted mindset about homosexuality in that era. (I was happy to hear he had gotten some action. I realize this sounds inappropriate, but I *was* very happy to hear this. We were close. So I thought, *Oh, good*.)

Mr. O'Neill had also known about my dad's sexuality. I think Mr. O'Neill may really have been the only person I knew whom he'd told before Steven Levy. It had been an element of their close friendship.

"Did you and Mr. O'Neill . . . ?"

"Bill loved me but I didn't feel that way about him."

We talked about everything. I remembered one time in the '90s we'd seen a gay kiss on TV and my dad had said, "I don't think that is right, two men kissing."

And I'd replied, "I think that's right. I think that's *just right*."

Now I think my dad was born a generation or two too early. If he had been born in a different era, he probably would have had a boyfriend. He couldn't break out of what was expected of him as a Catholic growing up in Cleveland in the 1930s and '40s. And he never left Ohio.

I don't think my dad was attracted to Mr. O'Neill. He had so many complicated feelings about being a homosexual. He had a self-hatred for being attracted to men. It was against God's will. He wrote on a yellow pad of paper, "Why, God?"

But they had a deep beautiful friendship.

And on one of my first trips back to Cleveland from NYU, I remember describing all my fellow theater students to him and Mr. O'Neill by saying, "*Everyone's* gay!"

It felt real and exciting. "Everyone is gaaaaaaaaay—and everyone is coming out, tap dancing!"

I just felt, like, *This is fantastic*.

New York City was so different from Cleveland. When

Debbie Palermo's roommate's mom told Mrs. Palermo that Debbie was gay and that she didn't want her daughter to be "living with a sinner," Mrs. Palermo threw the phone across the room—because she was upset Debbie didn't tell her first. Her roommate's mom had told her before Debbie could tell her, and she was shocked because she wanted to defend Deb.

Debbie told me, "My mom's so upset I didn't tell her first and that she had to hear it from some judgmental mom."

I was glad that there were so many boys at NYU who were suddenly coming out of the closet and announcing they were gay. I loved being in an atmosphere that was liberal and artsy and where everybody could find themselves. I wanted to subconsciously push them with this information. To test them and see how they would react.

My dad and Mr. O'Neill said, "*Really?*"

They *loved* hearing about it.

MR. O'NEILL HAD DIED eight years before I finally had this full, open conversation with my dad in Ojai.

My dad had been on a trip to Prague, but, as he said, "the Holy Spirit was guiding me and told me to cut the trip short."

Mr. O'Neill had gotten so thin by that time.

When my dad came back, he went straight to Mr. O'Neill's house and told him, "The rescue squad is coming over." Mr. O'Neill complained that he wasn't ready but my dad said, "They are coming anyway."

Once Mr. O'Neill was in the hospital, my dad visited all the time. He discovered that Mr. O'Neill's house and finances were in terrible shape.

Mr. O'Neill confessed that he had not collected the rent from his tenant for four years.

He said, "Oh, what is wrong with me, Jim?"

My dad said, "Oh, Bill!"

On one of these visits, he and Mary brought Mr. O'Neill a TV set. But as they were carrying it through the hospital a nurse told them, "I'm sorry, he's expired."

And my dad said, " '*Expired*'?"

They hadn't even called to tell him.

Gay people have fought for these things for so long.

My dad said, "Bill always knew that he would die before me, because he would say things like 'Jim, when I go, lay me out well. Give me a good one.' "

Mary and I both flew home to Cleveland. The day of the funeral, we had to stop at the mortuary to pay our last visit before they closed the casket. My dad looked devastated. First he kneeled and said some prayers. Then he stood up and looked in. Watching him, his shoulders seemed so little. His feet did, too. He put his hand on Mr. O'Neill's hand. Then we left the room and drove to the cemetery in a rented limo. My dad was a little grumpy in the car. There were twelve people who actually came to the cemetery. It was cold and gray. The priest said a few words. My dad stood alone—closest to the casket. I saw my dad's friend Anne Doyle sobbing. She had dated Mr. O'Neill a long time ago.

I cried a lot . . . because my dad lost his best friend of fifty years . . . and because I was worried about what he would be like when the pain really set in.

Then we got back into the limo and talked about where you go after death.

My dad said what he'd always said since Mary and I were little: "When you're Catholic, when you die, you don't die. You have eternal life."

As a girl I remember asking him, "What's eternal life?"

And he told me, "You live forever and ever and ever in heaven."

Now Mary said, "The thought of forever and ever and ever and ever makes me dizzy."

I would spin around in circles in our living room teasing my hair, thinking, *Foreverandeverandeverandeverandeverandeverandeverandever* . . . Until I thought, *This feels like too much to wrap my head around.*

I didn't like thinking about eternity.

Now my dad told us, "I'm not sure where you go, but I know that God takes care of you."

Back on Winchell Road, he invited people over for drinks and sandwiches—the Irish tradition. Mary and I saw him pour himself a drink and cringed. He had been sober for a long time.

Once he started drinking, he said, "I should have been tougher on Bill," as if it were his fault that he was dead.

Then he told us he had had this dream about our mom.

"I said to her, 'Look what beautiful daughters you have! You've missed them growing up!' But she would never talk back."

He asked me, "Molly, are you aware that I substituted you for Peg after she died? You are just like your mother and I was wrong to do that but you knew what was going on and you were such a good sport about it and I'd take you to wakes and dinner parties and even though you wanted to be with your friends you went along with it."

I said, "Yes."

And he seemed surprised.

It wasn't the first time we'd had this conversation. Once we'd watched an *Oprah* special on that subject—parents who make their children into surrogate spouses—and he'd said, "I feel like I did that to you.

"I loved your mother so much and you are just like her."

I'D NEVER SEEN MY dad cry as much as he cried that day. He kept saying how lucky I was that I had such good, supportive friends in LA, where I was still waitressing and working on my stage show. He said that my roommate, Brian Donovan, was "the best. The finest." And he cried as he said it. "'The finest' should be triple underscored! *Triple underscored.*" Then he added, "It's too bad the funeral couldn't have been in California, because you could have packed the house, Molly. Bill would have liked that."

Ann Ranft came over and said she thought it was sad that my dad was drunk because he had just lost his best friend. The next morning my dad woke up with a terrible hangover and told us, "I never want to drink again."

BEFORE MARY AND I flew back to New York and LA, we went out to dinner and he asked us, "Who of all the people at the wake do you think made me feel the best?"

Before we could answer, he told us, "John Goulet."

The counterman at Sand's Deli, who'd always been so nice to us. My dad said that a few months earlier John Goulet had seen Mr. O'Neill "drunk as a skunk" at a Van Aken bar, despondent over a falling-out with my dad and "bawling like a baby" as he told John how much he loved my dad, how he was so lucky to have him, and that if anything happened, he wouldn't know what to do without him.

As my dad told us all this, his face tightened up so he could hold back his tears—but they came out anyhow.

I also wanted to cry but I held myself tightly. I wanted to be strong. I couldn't let myself go until I'd left Cleveland and was up in the air, listening to Rickie Lee Jones on a plane back to LA, hiding my face so the seat next to me wouldn't know I was crying, thinking, *Just twenty-five years ago my mom, sis, and cousin died.*

Death brings up so much. All the love and truth can pour out at the end.

When I got back to LA, I talked to my dad on the phone.

He said he'd just watched *Jeopardy!* and he couldn't believe that he couldn't pick up the phone to call Bill like he always did. He said he was still in shock about the whole thing.

He said he was disappointed that none of his siblings had come to the funeral and that only twelve people showed up at our house.

"I wish there could have been more for Bill," he said.

He said he would pray for them but that it was going to be hard to get over.

I told him that he should move to LA. He said, "Yeah. Maybe I'll get a little apartment or something."

NOW MORE THAN A DECADE had passed since he'd lost Mr. O'Neill.

After my dad and I had our big talk at Carrows diner, Alison, who had always been so close to my dad, came down from Santa Barbara and met us for dinner at Suzanne's, this Italian restaurant in Ojai.

It was her birthday and my dad told Alison, "It's all on Paramount Pictures."

Alison had always totally gotten the silly side of my dad. And my dad kept saying it was on Paramount—since Paramount Pics *was* paying for everything! We had the time of our lives, laughing until late. The whole evening was like a dream.

Later, though, my dad told me that his favorite part of the whole trip was sitting at Carrows diner, just me and him, talking. I was happy for him that he had finally felt able to come out to me. He never got to come out to his friends or his immediate family. I'm so glad that I asked the question. I'm so glad that he answered. I'm so glad that he'd *wanted* to answer.

I feel that everything happened the way it was supposed to happen. I'm even happy he showed up drinking that final *SNL* night, because it set into motion pivotal conversations and allowed us to have those final wonderful months where so much was revealed and shared.

MY DAD'S NEIGHBOR ON Winchell Road told me that a few months after our big talk in Ojai, "Your dad put up Christmas lights in the window for the first time ever. Boy, did they look beautiful."

CHAPTER 21

Small Parts

WE WERE ON THE PHONE FOR EIGHTY-SIX MINUTES the last time we talked. It was such a good conversation. I was so lucky that I had left *SNL,* because we got to talk so much more than we would have been able to if I had still been busy with the show. He was glad I had left. He didn't want me to be working so hard. I didn't bring up what we had talked about in California. It was a big thing to tell. I figured if he wanted to talk about any of that again, I would let him lead. He must have thought all about our conversation at the Four Seasons. I could tell because what he said to me was this: "The best thing that I ever did was to have you girls. You and Mary. That's the best thing I ever did." And then he said, "I just want you to know you're my lucky star."

"Thank you," I said. "Thank you!"

He really wanted me to know that.

And in a letter he told me, "You and Mary are my best buddies and always will be. My love for you and Mary will always continue and any problems either of you have I want to be there to show you my deep love and console you both and comfort you and understand you in any and every way I can."

THEN WE HAD A quick conversation four days later, on a Saturday afternoon, before he went to a family wedding. He was a little worried about money.

He said, "Assisted living can be $6,000 a month; times twelve that's $72K."

I told him he should come to New York City and live in the studio I owned.

He didn't want to do that.

I invited him to California.

He said he would think about it and get back to me.

And he started weeping.

A FEW HOURS LATER, at the wedding, he suddenly put too much pressure on one of his legs—and cracked his femur. He was at his best, stone sober, making the rounds, talking to everyone, being his charming, sweet self, and then *crack*.

The prostate cancer had advanced enough to spread into the bone.

"If he had not taken Lupron, it would have spread to the bones faster," George's boyfriend, Larry, told me later. "Lupron kept him alive. But when you break a bone and you have cancer and your immune system is compromised because you are suddenly immobilized, you get pneumonia in the hospital and then you get a staph infection and it kills you."

When he arrived at the hospital, he was afraid his family was going to spread rumors about what had happened at the wedding. He did not want people thinking he had *fallen* or that he had been drinking.

No misinformation.

He just stood up the wrong way and the femur cracked.

My dad would have liked to have gotten away from some members of that big family.

And into piano bars.

I WAS WAITING FOR my dad to call back to let me know if he'd decided to come to California. It seemed like days had passed and I had not heard back.

Then I got a call from Aunt Bernie, saying "Your dad is not good. He's in the hospital. He doesn't want you to know. He doesn't want you to worry." But his oncologist told Aunt Bernie she should call us girls.

I PACKED MY BAGS fast and caught a cab to JFK, listening to "Back in Black" on my headphones to soundtrack the urgency I felt heading to the airport.

He went into the hospital and he never came back out. He was there for five days total. By the time I got there, he couldn't talk much. He was coughing a lot.

My dad did not fear dying. He *was* a rebel and a radical. He felt like he had lived a good life. He was ready to die. So when cancer took him, he didn't mind.

"I don't want to live and be really old and dependent," he said.

He'd smoked cigarettes because he didn't want to live to be too old. That tape-recorded conversation with his doctor wasn't the only time he said he had a death wish.

"I'm so ready. I've lived such a good, full life," he said. He was seventy-two.

He had done as much as he wanted to do. He'd said everything he needed to say.

He caught pneumonia in the hospital and was coughing all the time. I wanted to bring him salt water so that he could gargle and get some relief. I left his room to get a big cup of it.

Salt! Salt! Salt! That's gonna get all that shit out of there.

The salt water helped him more than anything. The next day I brought him more packs of salt but by then it was clear that the salt was no longer going to help.

Though he was still trying really hard to speak, even to make jokes.

At one point, when they were moving him every which way to take X-rays, he finally told the technicians, "If you guys don't stop, I'm going to call 911! Get me out of this hospital!"

He said he didn't want any visitors. Just Mary and me. Though eventually he made an exception for Ann Ranft and Mrs. Ranft. And he asked about Steven Levy a lot. Then he fell asleep. As I was sitting quietly in the room while he slept, a nurse who worked in radiology came and sat next to me.

She said, "I know your dad. He comes in to get his Lupron shots and he's always dressed up in a suit with a tie. He talks about you and Mary all the time. Telling me all about you two."

"He does? He dresses up and wears a tie when he comes in for his Lupron?"

She told me she did in-home care work and I asked for her number.

I was still thinking he was going to come home. My sister knew he wasn't coming home. But I was still in denial—wanting to do anything and everything I could to get him better. I couldn't accept it.

The nurse had to take me out of the room and say, "He's dying. This is it."

HAD I NOT QUIT the show, I would not have had that time for that phone call with him. I wouldn't have had those eighty-six minutes to talk. When people ask me if I regret leaving *SNL,* I say no, because if I had not left, I never could have had that conversation on the phone. I would have been too busy—like a doctor, always on call. That was my last big conversation with him. I fucking got it in the end. It was like a miracle. It was beautiful. I'm a spiritual person and it could not have gone better.

Just because he admitted he was gay or bi didn't mean that he didn't love being a father to Mary and me. He wanted me to understand how much he loved that he got to be our dad! During that phone call he was able to really talk. Once he was in the hospital, he could barely speak, so thank God we had that long talk. I don't take things like that for granted. Not everyone gets this in death.

This is the gift I will carry in my heart. After he died, I looked at all my old phone bills, seeing exactly how many minutes I'd talked to him in those last few months—ninety minutes there, thirty minutes there, fifteen there. I wanted to make sure that he'd felt loved. I would obsess about it. I graphed it like a math problem. I highlighted all my phone bills, looking at the minutes we talked. Made charts. Wrote it all out in a notebook, wanting *proof.*

It was part of my grieving. The more I graphed, the more comfort I felt.

I held his hands in the hospital room. He was dying. *These sweet hands have done so much for me for the last thirty-seven years,* I thought.

My dad would wave to me from our big front window every single time I left the house as I walked up the street.

Every.

Single.

Time.

We would keep waving back and forth as I walked up Winchell Road until I was out of sight.

I FELT INCREDIBLY HONORED to be there while he was dying.

I had lost my mom so abruptly. I treasured the good ending with my dad. That the rug was not pulled out from under me so suddenly. That I had time to say goodbye.

AFTER BEING RUSHED TO the hospital, my dad almost immediately developed a staph infection. It spread quickly to his lungs and kept him from being able to talk for more than a few sentences at a stretch. So that phone conversation really was the last time we talked.

He gave Mary and me a bunch of advice on the day that he died.

He was speaking so softly, we could hardly hear him. "I want to be hooked up to the morphine," he said. "But first let me give you girls advice. So, Molly, get married to Fritz, because it's a good thing to get married—don't delay. You need to have children, because that's the greatest thing you could ever do in life." He knew I wanted to be a mom. "Get married and go on," he said. "Don't cry for me, because I'll be happy"

"Will you watch over us from heaven?" we asked.

"Indeed," he said.

Now Mrs. Ranft was taking photos of him while he was dying.

They brought in the morphine, and we knew once he'd had that, he was going to be slipping away. He knew what was happening and began saying his very last words. He could barely talk. Before he could begin speaking, he had to take a big hit of oxygen. So he'd do this deep breath—"Aaaahhh . . ."—and then speak.

First he said, "Get along—you and Mary, get along."

My dad was a fan of this one movie I'd been in called *Analyze This*. Billy Crystal played a therapist and I was one of his patients, Caroline, who had just been through a breakup and was crying all through her session. At the end of the hour the therapist tried to kick me out and I told him that he was just like my ex.

Then he said, "Caroline, you know that's not true. I'm going to see you next week, whereas Steve *never* wants to see you again."

My dad just loved this little scene.

So he took a big inhale of oxygen to give some more advice, and we leaned in . . . we could hardly hear him.

"Aaaahhh . . ." And then he said, "Small parts."

"Okay. Small parts: Yeah?" we repeated, trying to make out what he was saying.

Then he took another deep inhale of oxygen and said, "Aaaahhh . . . In movies."

So now we repeated, "In movies: Yeah?"

Then he took a final deep inhale:

"Aaaahhh . . . Like *Analyze This*."

And then he died.

I'm not kidding.

HIS FINAL ADVICE WAS: Don't ever underestimate a good, small part in a movie like *Analyze This*. There are no small parts.

That was literally the last thing.

And he was flatline dead.

As we sat there in silence over my father's body, for some reason Ann Ranft's mom asked a completely random question: "Molly, who was that guy you dated and broke up with?"

And with that my dad rose up from the bed. We *thought* he was dead. Now he made a sound like "Bwaahrrrrrrrarrgghhh!"—one hand up in the air fingers spread out like a claw. And then he went back to the dead.

Because a boy had hurt his little girl and my dad knew. My dad cursed an ex-boyfriend on his deathbed. He was dead and he came back to life for me.

I GOT IN TOUCH with my dad's oncologist to thank him for having Aunt Bernie call Mary and me to the hospital when he did. If he hadn't told my aunt to call us, I don't know if we would have made it to the hospital. He said my dad knew it was time. He said, "It was a blessing he died when he did. He would've been in a lot of pain. No radiation—that was his choice. He was totally clear of mind, not delirious or incompetent."

After my dad died, so many people called and sent letters and flowers.

Eugene Pack, Alison Earle, Steve Koren, Deb and Mike Palermo, Jimmy Whalen from Cravings, George Cheeks, Drew Barrymore, Cheri Oteri, Adam Sandler and Jackie Sandler, Robert Smigel, Matt Piedmont, Lyn Henderson, Lisa Sundstedt, Jimmy Fallon, Marci Klein, Will Ferrell and Viveca Paulin-Ferrell, Rob Muir, and so many others.

I wrote down what Lorne said: "Molly, I'm terribly sorry—it's an odd thing because this is the anniversary of my own father's death. It's terribly sad. But I know nobody made a parent prouder than your dad. He got to see you flourish and blossom."

AT HIS FUNERAL we played Judy Garland's "Battle Hymn of the Republic," as he had requested.

My dad had written this on a yellow legal pad:

God is love. God is nature. God is the sun, the moon and the stars and all the planets and the outer universe. God is more than our feeble brain could ever conceive.

God is the light.

CHAPTER 22

Motherhood

O NCE, WHEN MY KIDS, STELLA AND NOLAN, WERE LITTLE, I took them Halloween shopping at Target.

When we came outside, our car was *gone.*

"Hey, our car is not here!"

Oh, no! I thought, *My car got towed.*

I didn't want to scare them. I thought, *I'm the leader. I can't act panicked.* So I decided to make it a mystery we needed to solve.

My kids were sort of in shock and replied, "Oh, no, Mommy! What are we going to do?"

I said, "It's okay. This is actually *exciting.* It's going to be an adventure. This is a good thing that has happened, because it is going to lead us down an interesting path, so let's just be open and see where it takes us."

It took them a while to get with the intrigue, and I had to hold back my own worry, but pretty soon we were all really into it, carrying around these mummies, skulls, and skeletons, until we saw one of those Bureau of Street Services trucks parked down the street. *Yessssss!*

I knocked on the window and said, "If my car were theoretically towed, do you know where they put it?"

The driver said, "Oh, your car probably got towed since it's rush hour now! They would probably bring it over to Hollywood Tow."

Then he did a double take and said, "Can I ask you . . . are you who I think you are?"

I nodded my head yes.

"You were in *Superstar*? Get in here! I'll help you!"

So we all enthusiastically hopped into his truck. He let my kids play with the lights on the roof while he took us all to Hollywood Tow, with our mummies and dummies tossed in the bed.

Once we got there he asked, "Are you okay? Do you have enough money? I can sit here in my truck and wait for you till you make sure your car is in there."

Go get the car. Write the check. They never saw Mommy sweat.

Obviously, this whole situation was helped by the fact that he had recognized me. But I resolved that my kids would learn that this stuff happens in life, and what matters is your attitude and how you handle it. There's no need to get upset: Go get the car, write the check, get back on the road. Maybe it happened for some reason and maybe the fact that this happened is some sort of protection. Who knows? They told everyone at school the next day, "Our car got towed! We got to ride in a truck! We got to do the lights!" It turned out to be the best day.

Another time I was driving Stella and Nolan and Nolan's friend Bobby to Bobby's favorite restaurant, CPK, when I ran out of gas.

Nolan said, "Don't worry, Bobby. This happens all the time."

Bobby said, "This has happened before?"

Ha, ha. Yes.

But it was hectic—there were cars zooming by and we were all really hungry.

Then Nolan said, "No, guys! It's a fun adventure, you'll see!"

At which point somebody pulled over. This nice guy who just helped us.

I pointed out, "Most people are good. And then you get to meet this nice stranger and he's like an angel or something, and for some reason maybe this is meant to be."

I hope that my kids will see when they are adults not to stress out—that this stuff happens. It's part of life. It's how you handle it.

In both cases I thought, *This is because of my dad.*

One morning both my kids were tired and didn't seem ready to go to school.

I said, "All right, all right, we can be late. It's fine." So we all had what we call a "Slow Start." We stopped at the Griddle, had French toast, talked, and took turns taking items off the table and making the others guess what we'd removed. We had fun.

After a while I asked, "Now are you guys ready to go to school?"

And they were.

It's good to be responsible, but there's no point in being so stressed that you can't adjust or bend the rules a little when necessary. Particularly when dealing with your kids. I'd rather send them to school happy and relaxed than send them to school when they aren't quite ready.

That all comes from Jim Shannon.

A FEW YEARS AGO I was cast in the role of a mother who's dying of cancer. The movie was called *Other People*, and it was written by the brilliant Chris Kelly, a former head writer at *SNL*. It was his first screenplay and his directorial debut. And it's semi-autobiographical. His mother's life was cut short by cancer. And it was an honor to play her.

I could tell she loved being a mother, and that she was strong and funny. There's a beautiful scene where Jesse Plemmons, the actor playing my son, says to his mother as she's dying, slipping away, "I want to take you on a trip. I want to take you all around the world."

They're lying in bed, and she's very sick.

My character replies, "I get to see my whole world at dinner tonight. My kids, my family—that's my whole world."

And that line takes my breath away, because it is exactly how I feel, too.

I FEEL SO LUCKY. I got four and a half years with my mom on earth. I'm grateful I got that time with her. It's substantial and thank God I had that. Losing my mom at such a young age gave me this urgency—like, *This is it: you are up to bat, baby!* Because you never know how much time you're going to have with someone. It gave me a sense of gratitude for the time on earth you do have with people.

I don't take *any* of it for granted.

I love being a mom to Stella and Nolan. I truly feel like I hit the jackpot getting to be their mom. And some of the stuff that people complain about as far as parenting goes I can't relate to. I just think, *They are alive. We are all alive. Nobody is dead.* I think that a lot: *There is nothing to be upset about. We're alive!*

GETTING TO BE HERE with my kids, in a way that my mom wasn't—getting to do all the things for my kids that she never got to do because her life was cut short—is profoundly healing.

So the script of *Other People* hit me deeply in many ways.

My character tells her children, "All I ever wanted was to be a mother, and I got to do that three times."

When I read that script, I read that line and I thought: *Yes. I relate to this so deeply, with my heart and my soul.* All I ever wanted was to be a mother, ever since I was playing Family on the playground in Ohio, telling all the other kids, "I'm the mother. I'm gonna be the best mother."

I ALWAYS ASK Stella and Nolan, "Do I seem like a stressed-out mom or a happy mom?"

And they say, "You seem happy."

ACKNOWLEDGMENTS

I WOULD LIKE TO EXPRESS GRATITUDE TO THE FOLLOWING people:

First and foremost, I would like to thank my collaborator, Sean Wilsey. It started with "Let's generate some pages," and then you immediately had a vision for the whole book. I love how you and David Kurlander would make up songs about Jim Shannon. I learned from you that chronology can be overrated. You are so talented, Sean. A million thanks. Does that make sense?

Thanks to my literary agent, Kim Witherspoon at InkWell Management. Thank you for your guidance, toughness, patience, humor, and intelligence. And Maria Whelan—you are a dee-light.

Thanks to my editors extraordinaire, Daniel Halpern and Gabriella Doob. I appreciate how passionate both of you have been since day one. Dan, thanks for talking things out on the phone and giving me the smartest advice. You are a legend and a joy. Gabriella, thanks for your unwavering support and enthusiasm. I am grateful for your steadiness and calm always. You keep everything moving forward and always with such grace and kindness. You are pure gold.

Thanks to the entire HarperCollins/Ecco team especially

Helen Atsma, Miriam Parker, Meghan Deans, Caitlin Mulrooney-Lyski, Lydia Weaver, Michelle Crowe, Cindy Achar, and Allison Saltzman.

Andrew Jacobs for your excellent legal advice.

Robert Abele for getting me started on this writing journey, listening to all my stories, and being so sweet and supportive. You made me feel so safe. It was easy opening up to you.

I am enormously grateful to my friends who read drafts of my manuscript. Alison Earle Doub, thank you for your insight and intelligence and silliness. You loved my dad. Thank you for all your excellent notes. You were way ahead of everyone in understanding literature when we were in grade school. I knew how smart you were then. Thanks for getting me so excited about the book and all your support.

Ann Ranft, thanks for reading the manuscript and letting me share our childhood stories. Making up characters started with you.

Steve Koren, you are always there for me. I am forever grateful. Thanks for your help on the book. You are so special to me, Steve.

Chris Kelly, I treasure your encouragement. I deeply appreciate your perspective on the book. Your support means the world to me (and thanks Chris and Sarah Schneider for helping me settle on a title for the book after Allison Saltzman pitched *Hello, Molly!* and thanks, Allison, for designing the jacket cover).

To my manager and friend, Steven Levy. You are family. I've been working with you for so long and I still get so excited when I see you calling. Thanks so much for reading my manuscript and sharing your stories.

Debra Palermo: You guided me through this book and

made elements I was struggling with crystal clear. A million thanks, Deb, for your astute eye.

Mike Palermo, you are so wise. You cut to the truth always.

George Cheeks. Thanks for believing in the book and always having my back and for reading the book multiple times! It means so, so much to me. I think I'll miss you most of all, scarecrow.

Mike White, thanks for reading the book. Your support means everything to me and thanks for helping me out at a critical time and for teaching me that vague sentimental writing isn't good writing. I admire your bravery as a writer and take what you say very seriously. You always make me feel better and say just the right thing.

Madeleine Olnek, thanks for your superb notes. Thanks for telling me about the Dignity Catholics and for asking me to play the first-ever-onscreen queer Emily Dickinson in your movie *Wild Nights with Emily*.

Bryan Smyj, my stuntman, thanks for being so protective of me all those years. I appreciate you letting me interview you for the book. You tell a story like no one else.

Huge thanks to the resourceful, reliable Laurie Berdan at *SNL*. Thanks for all your thorough research.

To Lisa Sunstedt and Pretty Funny Women—thanks for interviewing me for your class, Lisa, and for your support always.

Arden Myrin, you helped me so much in the beginning before I even had a proposal, showing me the ropes, answering all my questions, and guiding me.

Joanna Parson, thanks for your transcription.

Thank you to Edie Baskin for the phenomenal photographs.

Mary Ellen Matthews, thanks for your wonderful photographs and help. SNL is so fortunate to have you.

Margot Hand, you believed I had a book in me way at the beginning.

Cynthia D'Aprix Sweeney, thanks for your priceless guidance during this process. I take notes when you talk and save your excellent emails.

Mike White, thanks for helping me out at a critical time and for teaching me that vague sentimental writing isn't good writing. I admire your bravery as a writer and take what you say very seriously. You always make me feel better and say just the right thing.

Adam Resnick, you are just the best! You helped me so much on the book at a time when I really needed you. Thanks for always being there for me at the perfect time. I am forever grateful to you, Adam!!!

John Goulet, thanks for letting me interview you. I cherish that call. It was easy to soak up what you were saying about your Corky and Lenny days as a counterman because as I told you—you have the voice of a professional broadcaster! Thanks for reminding me that it was my dad who brought you to your first meeting. You told me the first person God put in your path was my dad and how he said to you: "Don't worry, John. It's gonna be okay. We can help you and get you back on the right track. All is not lost." And my dad would ask you, "John what are you gonna do tomorrow?" You were unsure and my dad would say: "You are gonna go to another meeting and I am going to pick you up." Thanks for sharing these incredible stories.

To my fabulous publicity team: Melissa Kates, Bria Schreiber, and Sergio Tapia. Thank you for all your hard work on behalf of this book. You guys are the A-team!

And to the wonderful Dennis Kao, Sean Beiler, and Suzanne Mitchell for making my audiobook.

To my agents: Shani Rosenzweig, Jonathan Weinstein, and Mike Jelline and the United Talent Agency. And Jason Richman, thanks for introducing me to Kim Witherspoon in the first place.

To my dynamic legal team: Steve Warren and Huy Nguyen. Steve, your enthusiasm means the world to me. You are a force. Huy, thank you so much. You are just the best.

Rob Muir, thanks for helping me with this book and taking the time to share your perspective. I'm so glad I met you so many years ago at that improv class.

Also, thanks to our fellow writer-performers in the Rob and Molly show so many years ago, Liza Coyle Murray and Alex Herschlag.

In writing about a part of my life I may have left out people who were really important to me so on that note, special thanks to all of you.

Karolyn McKenzie, thanks for organizing everything and for your keen writer's eye. You made all the material so accessible.

Lorne Michaels, you changed my life. Thanks for giving me the break of a lifetime. I could talk to you endlessly.

Marci Klein, thanks for coming to my stage show all those years ago and for being so sweet to my family and for your help with this book and just everything.

I also want to thank Eugene Pack, David Kurlander, Matt Piedmont, Andrew Shaifer, Heather Graham, Fred Wolf, Bill Neill, Aubrey Plaza, Portland Helmich, Barbara Earle, Lyn Alicia Henderson, Nicole Venables, Tim Long, Maureen Entrup, Shira Lee Shalit, Megan Mullally, Lauren Pomerantz, Elaine Solloway, Elizabeth Clark-Zoia, Amy Brooks,

Dayle Reyfel, John MacInnis, Addie Tavormina, Renee Stahl Dektor, and Sandy Jones. You all helped me with this book in various ways.

And just a general thanks to all my amazing friends who have supported me along the way. You know who you are. I want to list everyone but then I'm worried I will forget and leave someone out. I like everyone to be happy so this is the safest route.

M: I am eternally grateful to you for EVERYTHING. Thank you for encouraging me to go toward the love and to embrace my life. Thanks for teaching me how turn my back on emotionally harmful people. You have helped me tremendously. Thanks for reading several drafts of my manuscript. Your blessing means everything to me.

Thanks, Aunt Bernie.

God bless you, Fran.

Uncle Hugh, thanks for sharing all your memories about my mom when you were alive.

And to my sister, Mary: Thank you for allowing me to share some of your memories in my book. I really appreciate it. You are my big-hearted sister and I love you! We survived these challenges together.

Thanks, Shannon, Clare, Jack, and Brian.

A very special thank-you to my wonderful husband, Fritz Chesnut. Thanks for reading the manuscript and for being so incredibly sweet and supportive the entire time and for really believing in me and the book. Thanks for reassuring me when I needed it most. You have been incredible. Fritz, you taught me how to smile! (JKJKJK—just wanted to make you laugh.) Seriously though, I love it when you shake your hips and make up silly dances for me. There is nothing better.

To my children, Stella and Nolan. You are my everything.

I feel so lucky I get to be your mom. I love you, I love you, I love you. What an honor it is for me to get to see you growing up. I feel so fortunate I have gotten to live way beyond the years my mom lived. It is deeply healing and profound and I do not take one second of it for granted. Stella and Nolan, you are my heart, my world.

To my mom and Katie, I carry you in my heart forever.

Mommy, I'm sorry you didn't get to watch us grow up. Thank you for passing on your love of books and reading. I hope I make you proud from heaven.

To my dad: I always felt deeply loved by you. You gave me so much confidence. You were nonjudgmental and way ahead of the times in inclusiveness. I loved your writing and performing. Thanks for always believing in me. You helped me develop into the person I am today. Thanks for always being so interested in everything I had to say. I miss laughing with you. I miss your silliness. I get so excited when you pop up in my dreams. I listen to Tom Petty's "Wildflowers" in my car when I drive around and think of you.

About the Author

MOLLY SHANNON is an actress and comedian. She spent six seasons as a member of the repertory company on *Saturday Night Live*, primarily known for the eclectic characters she created, such as Mary Katherine Gallagher and Sally O'Malley. In 2000, she received an Emmy nomination for Outstanding Individual Performance in a Variety or Music Program. In 2013, Molly received her second Emmy nomination for Outstanding Guest Actress in a Comedy Series for her work in *Enlightened* and again in 2018 for her portrayal of Val in NBC's award-winning comedy *Will & Grace*. In 2017, she was awarded the Independent Spirit Award for Best Supporting Actress for her performance in *Other People*, written and directed by *SNL* head writer Chris Kelly. Molly appears in HBO's series *The White Lotus*, created by frequent collaborator Mike White, and is currently starring in Chris Kelly and Sarah Schneider's Critics' Choice Award–nominated *The Other Two*. Molly was born in Shaker Heights, Ohio. She earned a BFA in drama from New York University's Tisch School of the Arts. She lives in California with her husband and two children.